10 TRUE TALES

D-DAY HEROES

Allan Zullo

SCHOLASTIC INC.

Dedicated to the memory of those heroes who gave their all—
especially those who made the ultimate sacrifice—on D-Day.
—A.Z.

ISBN 978-1-338-22265-4

10 9 8 7 6 5 4 3   18 19 20 21 22

Printed in the U.S.A.   40
First printing 2018

Book design by Cheung Tai

CONTENTS

OPERATION OVERLORD

I t was the largest invasion in history.

Known simply as D-Day, June 6, 1944, was a date like no other. A massive air-and-sea armada beyond anything the world had ever seen before powered across the English Channel in the dark of night, carrying more than 150,000 Allied troops. At dawn, the first assault wave of these brave soldiers, sailors, airmen, and Coast Guardsmen invaded the Normandy coast of Nazi-held France.

Here, on the beaches, atop the cliffs, between the hedge-rows, and in the fields, they sacrificed life and limb in a bloody, chaotic battle that marked the beginning of the end of World War II and German dictator Adolf Hitler's mad quest to rule the globe.

World War II had erupted after Germany, led by Hitler and the Nazi Party, invaded Poland in 1939. This caused Great Britain and France, who were allies of Poland, to declare war on Germany. Nazi forces then invaded and occupied Denmark, Norway, Belgium, Holland, Luxembourg, France, Yugoslavia, and Greece. Italy teamed up with Germany, and together they fought British forces in North Africa. By the summer of 1941, Germany had conquered most of Western Europe and then attacked the Soviet Union.

Meanwhile, on the other side of the world, Japan, which had invaded China in 1937, was trying to dominate East and Southeast Asia, despite protests from the United States. On December 7, 1941, Japan launched surprise attacks against several countries, including the American naval base at Pearl Harbor, Hawaii.

The United States had no choice but to declare war on Japan, Germany, and Italy—the three major countries that formed an alliance called the Axis powers. America joined the Allied powers, which included dozens of nations that opposed the Axis. The Allies were led by the United States, Great Britain, Canada, Australia, and the Soviet Union. The American military was forced to fight German and Italian armies in Europe as well as the Japanese military in the Pacific.

After devastating early setbacks, the Allies rallied and began winning ferocious battles in Europe and successfully invaded Nazi-occupied North Africa in 1942 and Sicily and mainland Italy in 1943. But to win the war in Europe, the Allies needed to invade German-held territory on the continent.

Hitler knew this and ordered the building of a virtual Atlantic Wall, a 2,400-mile-long series of fortifications, long-range guns, bunkers, land mines, and beach and underwater obstacles along the coast. What Hitler didn't know was where and when the invasion would occur. For months, the Allies carried out a clever scheme of deception to make the Germans think the Allies would strike at Pas-de-Calais, France, the closest town to Britain, just 60 miles across the Strait of Dover. The trickery included fake radio transmissions, double agents disclosing false information, and even the phony buildup of troops and equipment near Dover.

Meanwhile, in early 1944, the Allies were gathering in other areas of Britain to prepare for D-Day. (This name, by the way, was simply a common army term at the time indicating the start of any major military operation, but it is now enshrined forever to mean this particular invasion.) In the months leading up to D-Day, the Allies amassed troops, equipment, and supplies, and trained night and day in secret locations.

To head up the invasion, President Franklin D. Roosevelt chose General Dwight D. Eisenhower as Supreme Commander of the Allied Expeditionary Force. Under the code name "Operation Overlord," the plan called for Allied forces to cross the English Channel and strike along a 60-mile coastal stretch in a farming area of northern France known as Normandy.

The Americans would land on the beaches code-named "Omaha" and "Utah" while British and Canadian troops would attack the beaches known as "Gold," "Juno," and "Sword."

For the invasion on D-Day, the strength of the Allies' might was mindboggling: more than 5,000 vessels, including 1,100 warships and thousands of landing craft of all shapes and sizes; roughly 156,000 troops; and about 13,000 planes, including fighters, bombers, troop carriers, and gliders. And that was just for the first day.

Eisenhower chose June 5, 1944, as the date for the invasion, but stormy weather forced him to postpone it 24 hours. Although conditions were only slightly better (but still bad) on June 6—windy, 50s, cloudy—the invasion was a "go." Before the troops secretly left England, Eisenhower issued the Order of the Day. He said, in part: "You are about to embark upon the Great Crusade, toward which we have striven these many months. The eyes of the world are upon you. The hopes and prayers of liberty-loving people march with you. . . . You will bring about the destruction of the German war machine, the elimination of Nazi tyranny over the oppressed people of Europe, and security for ourselves in a free world. . . . I have full confidence in your courage, devotion to duty, and skill in battle. We will accept nothing less than full Victory!"

Shortly after midnight on June 6, 120 pathfinders parachuted behind enemy lines to place lights pinpointing the drop zones for the 13,000 fellow paratroopers who would follow within the hour. But because of heavy winds, low clouds, and German flak (bursting antiaircraft shells), many of the pathfinders' planes strayed off course. As a result, only 38 pathfinders came down near their drop zones. Others landed in fields, gardens, streams, and swamps miles away.

Similar problems plagued many paratroopers from the 82nd and 101st Airborne Divisions who jumped out of 822 troop-carrying planes and touched down far from designated drop zones. Wearing enormous amounts of gear, men drowned when they descended into swamps, flooded fields, and rivers. Others were riddled with bullets during their descent or died in planes that were shot down. Thousands were killed or wounded or couldn't find their outfits for days. Although widely scattered, the surviving paratroopers gathered in different units and started attacking the Germans, cutting communication lines, knocking out big guns, and capturing causeways.

Arriving in gliders before daylight, 5,000 British troops seized key bridges and roads, blocking any German reinforcements from reaching Gold, Juno, and Sword Beaches, which were not heavily defended. The troops stormed through German coastal strongholds to meet their objectives.

American troops from the 4th and 90th Infantry Divisions—many of them draftees and soldiers who had never been in combat—and the 4th Cavalry Regiment had similar success when they landed on nine-mile-long Utah Beach on the southeastern corner of the Cotentin Peninsula.

But the focal point of the Allied invasion—the six-mile stretch of Omaha Beach—turned into a horrific near-disaster for the 1st and 29th Infantry Divisions and US Army Rangers. The Germans took advantage of the cliffs and 100-foot-tall bluffs overlooking the beach to place antitank guns, artillery batteries, machine gun nests, mortar pits, and pillboxes (small concrete bunkers for shooters). The enemy spiked the beach with large metal obstacles, rolls of barbed wire, and land mines, and lined the waters just offshore with thousands of underwater mines and obstructions known as hedgehogs, which were designed to rip open the hulls of landing craft.

Among the first to reach the beach were US Navy underwater demolition teams tasked with blowing up the obstacles to create safe pathways for the arriving troops. But with little protection, most men on the teams were annihilated by German firepower, so only five lanes were cleared.

From several miles offshore, battleships and destroyers shelled the coastline while large transports transferred troops into smaller landing craft. Because of the heavy seas, the small boats rocked and rolled, drenching the occupants and making many seasick. Large swells swamped some vessels, which sank, drowning many men.

As landing craft neared shore, several hit submerged mines and blew up, flinging troops and equipment into the water. Enemy artillery and mortar rounds blasted vessels into smithereens.

Through the smoke, confusion, and strong currents, some boats landed miles off course. Many unloaded too far from the beach, causing troops to step off into water over their heads and drown because the weight of their backpacks and gear kept them from reaching the surface.

Dozens of trucks, bulldozers, and Sherman army tanks that were unloaded from landing craft sank like boulders when their flotation devices collapsed from the beating waves. Their crews went with them to the bottom.

Many of the troops who reached the sand were weak from

seasickness and slowed by their heavy, waterlogged clothes and gear. Finding little cover, they were slaughtered by machine guns spraying 1,200 bullets per minute. The wounded lay at the water's edge only to drown when the tide came in. Other than hiding behind beach obstructions, surviving troops found some cover behind a long shingle, a sloping embankment of small stones about 10 yards from the high-water line. But they couldn't stay there long because the Germans targeted them with mortar rounds.

The Allied casualty count was steep. According to the US National D-Day Memorial Foundation, 2,499 Americans and 1,914 troops from other Allied nations—a total of 4,413—were killed on the beaches of Normandy on D-Day. An estimated 6,000 were wounded.

Despite the carnage, the Allies persevered. By nightfall, many units had advanced, although it took five more days of fierce fighting to secure all the beaches. During that span, 326,547 Allied troops, 54,186 vehicles, and 104,428 tons of supplies had arrived.

In the following weeks, the Allies fought their way across the Normandy countryside. By the end of June, they had landed about 850,000 men and 150,000 vehicles and had seized the vital port of Cherbourg. By August, the Battle of Normandy was over.

The Allies continued their march through France and, after winning a series of brutal battles, ultimately drove the Germans out of Western Europe, liberating the once-conquered countries. On May 8, 1945—less than one year after D-Day—Nazi Germany signed an unconditional surrender. The war in Europe was over.

Following the dropping of atom bombs on the Japanese cities of Hiroshima and Nagasaki in August, the Empire of Japan formally surrendered on September 2, finally bringing World War II to an end.

The war, which involved more than 70 nations, resulted in the deaths of an estimated 60 million people, making it the deadliest conflict in recorded history. The men and women in the US military paid a dear price for victory: 406,000 killed, another 671,000 seriously wounded.

You are about to read 10 stories of incredible heroism on D-Day. These accounts—which use real names, dates, and places—are based on memoirs, oral histories, newspaper accounts, battle reports, and military files. An asterisk after a name means the person was real but the name was unknown. The book refers to navy and coast guard ships as "she" or "her" because it's an old maritime tradition that goes back centuries and is still a common practice.

You will see how the bold bravery, gritty determination, and fighting spirit of the forces of freedom reflected in the following stories transformed D-Day into the turning point of World War II.

THE SILENT
SKY WARRIOR

FLIGHT OFFICER GEORGE "PETE" BUCKLEY
74th Troop Carrier Squadron, 434th Troop Carrier Group

As Flight Officer Pete Buckley settled into the cockpit of his flimsy glider plane for his first combat mission, an unsettling thought crossed his mind: He might die within the next few hours.

The fresh-faced 19-year-old pilot was a member of a brash group of mavericks who were members of a stealth air force powered only by the wind and the courage of the men. They flew engineless aircraft towed by twin-propeller airplanes and then, after being released, they attempted to silently land—or, more likely, crash-land—behind enemy lines.

With no motors, no weapons, no parachutes, and no armor plating of any kind, these gliders were mockingly called "flying coffins." They were disposable and, to some extent, so were the pilots, who suffered a high casualty rate.

On this heart-pounding night, in the initial wave of gliders flying from England to Normandy, Buckley's job was to transport paratroopers, one heavy-duty weapon, and equipment through a hazardous curtain of enemy antiaircraft fire and land in German-occupied territory near Hiesville, France. If he was lucky enough to survive the landing—more than half of D-Day's 517 gliders would end up severely damaged or destroyed—he would have to grab his steel helmet and rifle and turn into a combat infantry soldier. Then he would have to make his way back to England so he could do it all over again in the following days.

The success of the invasion would depend, in large part, on the skill and bravery of the glider pilots and paratroopers who would be the first to reach Normandy before the Allies could storm ashore later that morning. If the glidermen and troopers could thwart the Germans from reinforcing the beaches, then victory was within reach.

That's what Buckley tried to focus on—victory. But the thought of death never left him.

Like thousands of other glider pilots in the US Army Air Forces, Buckley had been training for this moment for months in the United States and then in southeast England. None of the pilots knew when the invasion would take place, but they were itching to go, boasting about how they would "kick the Germans' butts."

In early June 1944, at an airfield outside the English village of Aldermaston, which was the home of his unit, the 434th Troop Carrier Group, Buckley sensed his fellow pilots' swagger was morphing into nervous excitement and tension. It certainly was for him. Arriving daily were hundreds of airborne troops, armament, and equipment. The military police were stationed at all gates and not allowing anyone in or out without special permission. *It could mean only one thing*, he thought. *D-Day is about to happen.*

On June 5, all tow-plane crews and glider pilots in his unit sat in the operations room for a briefing by the group's intelligence officer. He displayed a large map of Normandy and pointed to their objective—Landing Zone E in the fields around the village of Hiesville, five miles inland from Utah Beach. The pilots let out a low gasp. Buckley was one of them as he thought, *The time has finally come when we get to put our skills as pilots to the test.*

"Evidently the Germans know we're coming, so they're preparing a lively reception for us," said the officer. "Within the last forty-eight hours, they have been studding fields in the LZ with poles, which we're calling 'Rommel's asparagus.' [The poles were named after General Erwin Rommel, who was in charge of beefing up Germany's coastal defense.] Many of these poles are wired with explosives. Also, to prevent us from landing, the Nazis are flooding meadows and digging large ditches across fields."

An even bigger danger for the glidermen were the hedgerows—thick stands of tall trees that bordered the fields, many of which were so small they required a pinpoint landing. If a pilot came in too low, he would crash into the trees. If he came in too high, he would run out of room to land in the field and slam into the hedgerow at the far end.

"Because of our excellent flying record and our expertise shown in glider training exercises, we are going to lead the glider phase of the D-Day invasion," the officer announced. "In the first serial [wave], we're sending up fifty-two gliders carrying men and equipment of the 101st Airborne Division. The code name for this serial is 'Chicago.' Five minutes later, the 437th Troop Carrier Group from Ramsbury will tow another fifty-two gliders for the 82nd Airborne Division in the second serial. Their code name is 'Detroit.'"

Buckley had mixed emotions. On one hand, he was proud that the 434th would lead the way, but he also thought, *Maybe we shouldn't have been so good in our training operations.*

"Here's where it gets dicey," the officer continued. "We're carrying out this mission at night because the paratroopers who will be the first in can't wait until dawn to get the antitank guns, ammunition, medics, jeeps, and medical supplies that we will be bringing in. They'll need these things ASAP [as soon as possible], so that's what we'll do in the middle of the night."

As the room buzzed with murmurs, Buckley gulped. He looked around and noticed somber expressions had replaced the once eager gung-ho looks on the faces of his fellow glidermen.

Takeoff was scheduled for shortly after midnight, only a few hours away. *This is a tough pill to swallow,* Buckley thought. Most of their training had been for dawn or full daylight landings, with little nighttime practice. The thought of trying to land in enemy territory in the dark in strange fields with a heavily loaded glider sounded like a recipe for disaster.

After the briefing, Buckley and his copilot, Flight Officer Bill Bruner, went down to the flight line to check out their glider. Next, they went to the mess hall for what glidermen jokingly called "the last meal." Many who felt the need for spiritual assistance visited the chaplain, whose tent quickly filled to beyond capacity.

To prepare for the mission, Buckley and his copilot attached ammunition clips and hand grenades to their flight gear. They each carried a .45-caliber Colt pistol and a folding short-barreled automatic rifle called a carbine for use after what they hoped would be a safe landing.

Buckley's aircraft was to be the 49th in a formation of 52 gliders towed by 52 twin-engine C-47s. The gliders were gray-green, odd-looking, 48-foot-long Waco CG-4As, which had 84-foot wingspans. The skin was nothing more than special fabric stretched over a framework of steel tubing and plywood, yet the gliders each could carry nearly two tons of cargo and/ or troops. Buckley's glider would be hauling a maximum load— three members of the 81st Airborne Antiaircraft Battalion, ammunition, a 57mm antitank gun on wheels, entrenching tools, a camouflage net, boxes of rations, and other supplies.

About 30 minutes before takeoff, the tow planes' engines began to start up. Their loud coughing and throbbing reverberated across the field like an ominous, rumbling thunderstorm, which heightened Buckley's growing unease as he, Bruner, and the three troopers climbed aboard the glider. Everyone was putting on a brave face, which made Buckley ponder, *Are they that confident, or are they just as scared as I am?* He did his best to mask the fear that was churning his stomach and jangling his nerves.

In roughly three and a half hours, I might be dead, he told himself. *What did I get myself into? Why had I been so foolish as to volunteer for this job?* When he first joined the glider program right out of high school, none of the army brass at Dow Field in Bangor, Maine, had explained to him exactly what gliders would do in the war. Once he started training, he found out. It didn't bother him then because he had adopted the culture of devil-may-care glidermen who often thumbed their noses at regulations and danger. Oh, sure, more than 100 pilots died during training accidents, but it wasn't combat. All those practice flights were just that—practice.

Now this is the real deal, he told himself. The tow planes and gliders were lined up on each side of the field for nearly a mile. At 12:10 a.m., they began taking off. Soon it was tow plane No. 49's turn. It rolled down the runway through a light rain shower into the black of night. Suddenly, Buckley's glider, which was tethered to the C-47 by a 350-foot-long, three-quarter-inch-thick rope, jerked forward and was quickly airborne. As the wheels of the glider left the ground, one of the troopers in the back yelled, "Look out, Hitler! Here we come!" That triggered a few seconds of whoops and hollers before everyone turned mum.

All were thinking about the mission and their own mortality. *Well, there's no turning back now*, thought Buckley. He shoved aside his worries and concentrated on flying the glider, holding his position behind the C-47 at an altitude of 2,000 feet. It wasn't that easy. Because his glider was near the tail end of the large formation, it was getting buffeted by heavy turbulence caused by the prop wash of the tow planes, air pockets, and 40 mph winds. The fabric covering the fuselage beat against the glider's framework, creating an annoyingly harsh racket, too noisy to carry on a conversation. As for the four basic instruments on the control panel, they were so inaccurate he couldn't trust them. And, like most glidermen, he had no radio in order to maintain secrecy from the enemy. He also had to deal with the barrel of the large antitank gun that was poking into the cockpit between him and Bruner because it was the only way it could fit in the glider.

Buckley began to shiver. He wasn't sure if it was from the lack of any insulation in the glider to protect him from the damp, chilly air or from fear. Despite his discomfort, the darkness, turbulence, rain, and disorienting cloud banks, he kept his aircraft centered behind his tow plane, which was flying at about 125 mph throughout most of the flight. Aware that the longer he stared, the more likely his eyes would play tricks on him, he occasionally turned the controls over to Bruner for brief periods to give his eyes a rest.

Whenever the moonlight poked through the clouds, Buckley was awed by the sight of thousands of ships below steaming toward the French beaches. To him, the wakes looked like silvery, dainty ribbons.

Shortly after crossing the coast of France, the planes dropped to 600 feet. As those in the front of the formation passed over German positions, they awakened the enemy, who began firing at the invaders with antiaircraft weapons and small-arms fire. Because his glider was at the back of the formation, it encountered a heavier volume of flak and bullets than those up front. Buckley was both fascinated and frightened by the orange streams of tracer bullets and colorful antiaircraft fire streaking across the night sky. They reminded him of the Fourth of July, but there was nothing festive about them. *How can anything fly through this stuff and come out in one piece?* he wondered.

Bullets began ripping through the fabric of the glider, sounding like bursting popcorn. His glider was still attached to the rope, so there was little evasive action that he could take. As enemy fire intensified, Buckley hunched over to make himself as small as possible. He tucked his elbows in close to his body and pulled his knees together to protect vital parts. He was even tempted to take his feet off the rudder pedals so they wouldn't stick out so far—anything to make himself a smaller target. By now, he was sweating profusely as if he had been running a marathon.

Shortly after 4 a.m., the moment of truth arrived for Buckley. The green light on the tow plane's astrodome—a Plexiglas half sphere on the top of the C-47's fuselage—came on. That was the signal indicating they were over the landing zone, and it was time for Buckley to cut loose.

He hesitated because he couldn't see anything below him in the darkness other than tracer bullets. *Where am I going to land?* He wished he could remain tethered to the C-47, which would be turning around and heading out of danger and back to England. He also wished this were a scary dream that would end right now and he'd wake up safe and sound in bed. *Wishes don't count in combat*, he told himself. *Only doing what you're trained to do matters.*

He refused to release the tow rope. *This can't be the LZ.* His gut instinct told him to wait until he could see something—anything—below. The seconds ticked off. He knew if he delayed any longer, he could miss the landing zone altogether and end up even farther into enemy territory.

Taking a deep breath, Buckley cut loose. It was all up to him now. Coasting at 90 mph, he started a 360-degree turn to the left, feeling his way down into the black. He had never been so afraid in his life. *I know the ground is down there, but where is it?*

The glider kept descending as more bullets tore into it. "See anything, Bill?" he asked his copilot.

"Not yet," Bruner replied.

"We're about to run out of altitude."

What Buckley wouldn't know until hours later was the fate of other gliders. Dozens clipped buildings and tall trees or ended up in flooded meadows. Others landed safely, but as the troops and crew streamed out, they were machine-gunned to death. Many gliders were shattered or had their wings sheared off by Rommel's asparagus, spilling men and equipment all along the length of the fields. Several crashed into farmhouses, stone walls, and even cows.

Lieutenant Colonel Mike Murphy, the lead pilot in glider No. 1, had guided his aircraft onto a field, but it slid 800 feet along wet grass and smashed into a stand of trees at 50 mph. The devastating collision snapped the glider into pieces like matchsticks, breaking Murphy's legs and killing Brigadier General Donald Pratt, the highest-ranking American officer to die on D-Day.

Glider No. 51 crash-landed after its tow plane received a fatal hit from flak and spiraled in flames into a swamp five miles southwest of the landing zone. Lieutenant Raymond Howard, pilot of the stricken C-47, was fatally shot by the Germans as he crawled out from the burning wreckage. The rest of the men were taken prisoner.

In the darkness, amid the flak and tracer bullets, Buckley kept looking for a place to land, knowing time was running out. Finally, he glimpsed an open field bordered by trees. "Brace for landing!" he shouted.

Now came his next worry: Were there any obstacles he might hit? *The only thing I know for sure is that Germans are shooting at us, and they're going to be right there waiting when we climb out of our glider,* Buckley thought.

Whispering a prayer to himself, he straightened out his glide path (line of descent) and headed in. Stiffening his body for the expected impact, he flared his aircraft just above the stalling speed of 70 mph, barely slipped over the trees, and touched down. It was a perfect landing. "I can't believe it!" he crowed as the glider rolled across the field. "Smooth as glass. How lucky can you get?"

But just as he relaxed his muscles, he, Bruner, and the three troopers felt a tremendous bone-jarring crash. The glider had plowed into an unseen 12-foot-wide, 6-foot-deep ditch that the Germans had dug across the field. The glider toppled into the ditch nose first, skidded across the watery bottom, and slammed into the base of the other side, buckling the fuselage and splitting open the floor. Because the aircraft had been skimming along the ground so fast, its front section climbed partially up the opposite bank before it buried itself in the dirt.

For several seconds, Buckley, Bruner, and the troopers sat in stunned silence. "Is anyone hurt?" Buckley shouted. Everyone responded they were okay. "Good," he said. "Let's get out of here!" They exited quickly because rifle and machine gun fire were erupting in nearby fields. Fortunately, it seemed the Germans weren't aware of Buckley's cracked-up glider.

Suddenly, a flare lit up the surrounding area. That's when Buckley was surprised to see glider No. 50 resting—without a dent—across the ditch on the far side of the same field. It was carrying the jeep that was assigned to tow the antitank gun in

Buckley's plane. The men spent the next 30 minutes furiously digging the hinged nose of the glider out of the dirt until they could open it and roll out the weapon. Then they made a ramp into the ditch so the jeep could hook up the weapon.

While the men were working on the ramp, the US naval bombardment began pounding the area just beyond the beaches where the Allies would begin invading within the hour. Even though the shelling was five miles away from Buckley, the ground shook under his feet and the din from the explosions hurt his ears. "Let's say a few prayers for the kids who'll be storming the beaches," Buckley said. "They better be successful. Our lives are at stake."

At dawn, he and the others finally hitched the gun to the jeep, which then pulled it out of the ditch. While the rest of the men left to find their assigned units, Buckley clutched his carbine and went on foot alone to locate the 101st Division Command Post (CP) at Hiesville. Having completed his main mission, he felt a sense of pride and relief. Whatever fear he experienced on the flight had diminished as well. He had his swagger back.

Buckley was pleased that he had followed his instincts by waiting before he released the tow rope. If he had cut loose at the first signal from the tow plane, he would have landed miles from his designated landing zone instead of only a half mile away.

Walking along a dirt road between hedgerows, he stopped a jeep driven by a paratrooper from another unit who was also trying to find the CP. Buckley hopped on the hood and rode with him. About five minutes later, several German soldiers in nearby trees opened fire on them. Buckley rolled off the hood while the vehicle was still moving and was nearly run over. He hopped back in and after the two of them cleared the killing zone, he told the driver, "That's enough of that. I'm better off going on my own."

Shortly after the driver left, Buckley walked down the narrow lane and heard the sounds of a nearby firefight. Glancing to his left, he froze in fear. There, in an opening in the hedgerow about waist high, a rifle barrel was pointing directly at him. Unable to move by the terror of thinking he was about to die, Buckley waited for the fatal bullet to strike him. But nothing happened. The gun didn't fire. In fact, it didn't even move.

Snapping out of his self-induced paralysis, Buckley dived for cover, then crawled over to the hedgerow and cautiously peered through the bushes. On the other side, he saw a hand-built German bunker large enough for five or six soldiers. But there was only one man in there, and he was dead from several bullet wounds. The German's rifle was still poking through the thicket. *Thank God for the paratroopers who killed him earlier,* Buckley thought. *They probably left him in this position to scare others. Well, they succeeded in scaring the heck out of me.*

The incident made him much more cautious, and he began walking in a crouch while his head constantly swiveled. After an exchange of gunfire and ducking blasts from mortar rounds, Buckley encountered a German lying in a pool of blood at a dirt intersection. The soldier, who was barely alive and looked no older than the teenage pilot, had been hit by shrapnel. Buckley felt horrible watching the young German die. *There's nothing I can do for him.* It was still too early in the day for Buckley to have developed a deep hatred for the enemy. That would come later when he saw the gruesome handiwork of the Germans: bodies of British and American paratroopers who had been killed while trying to free themselves from tree-snagged parachutes.

As Buckley continued his trek toward the command post, he spotted an American paratrooper standing alone in the middle of a large meadow. *I wonder what he's doing out there. Maybe he can tell me where the CP is.* The gliderman approached him and noticed that he was wearing an army air forces flak vest.

After Buckley introduced himself, the paratrooper said, "Hey, thanks for coming out to help me, but I suggest you go find a flak vest to wear." When Buckley asked why, the soldier replied, "Some Kraut snipers are in the woods over there, and I'm trying to draw their fire so my buddies hiding off to the side can nail them."

Just then, a bullet buzzed Buckley's head, and he dropped to the ground. The paratrooper, who remained standing, said, "That's one of them now!"

Wishing him luck, Buckley picked himself up and beat a hasty retreat in search of a flak vest, but he had no luck finding one in the wreckage of nearby gliders. The paratroopers had snatched all the vests. *Walking around by myself probably isn't the smartest thing for me to do. I'm just asking for a sniper to knock me off.*

By late afternoon, after a few more close calls with sniper fire, Buckley arrived at the division's command post in Hiesville, where he and other glider pilots were assigned shifts to guard the perimeter in case the Germans tried to launch a counterattack.

Buckley was exhausted. Like most glider pilots, he had been awake for 36 straight hours, and strain and fatigue were setting in. Some soldiers walked like zombies, and others were sleeping on their feet. Buckley lay down on the ground in a courtyard and dozed off.

At 8:30 p.m., he and others returned to the fields to provide security for a serial of large British gliders known as Horsas, which were carrying needed vehicles, bulldozers, and weapons. Towed by C-47s from the 434th, they were expected to arrive at 9 p.m. When the gliders began their descent, the Germans, who had been patiently lurking in the hedgerows, opened up on the defenseless planes, sending several crashing in flames.

Buckley and his comrades engaged in a deadly firefight with the Germans but couldn't stop them from destroying Horsas in the air and on the ground. Without radios, the pilots had no way of knowing they were gliding into ambushes until it was too late. If they weren't shot out of the sky, the Horsas were smashing head-on into hedgerows because the fields were much too small for the big gliders. Several men were killed on impact and others were captured.

The carnage Buckley witnessed left him on the verge of tears. But he and his comrades fought valiantly until they drove off the Germans. After the splintered gliders were unloaded and the wounded and dead taken away, Buckley returned to the command post, where he dug a foxhole in an apple orchard behind a stable.

Curled up in his trench, he closed his eyes and recalled his boyhood days in Connecticut when he and the neighborhood kids played war with sticks as guns. It was always the Yanks vs. the Germans. *That was a lot of fun then,* he thought. *Now I'm playing war for keeps. This is not fun.*

The next day, Buckley helped herd hundreds of German prisoners to Utah Beach and then took a transport ship back to England. From there, he flew several more glider missions into Normandy and other regions of Europe until Germany was defeated.

After the war, he settled in Milford, Connecticut, where he enjoyed a long career as a professional photographer. He and his wife, Jeanne, raised two daughters and had four grandchildren and five great-grandchildren.

Like other glider pilots who participated in the Normandy landings, Buckley was awarded the Air Medal for his role on D-Day. The 434th also received a Distinguished Unit Citation, which stated, "The outstanding courage, skill, and fearless initiative demonstrated by all of the personnel of the 434th Troop Carrier

Group, both individually and as a closely knit combat team, contributed immeasurably to the success of the European invasion and materially accelerated the collapse of enemy forces on the Normandy coast."

The US Army Air Forces trained about 6,000 glider pilots during the war. Of those, 211 were killed in action, 636 were wounded, and 140 died in training accidents. The Waco CG-4A glider was mothballed after the war, and today fewer than a dozen have been restored by private citizens.

The brave glidermen proudly wore on their chests silver wings emblazoned in the center with the letter G. Technically, the letter stood for "glider." But the pilots were quick to tell everyone that the G actually stood for "guts."

This story is based, in part, on the recollections of George "Pete" Buckley, who granted permission to use material from his article "Normandy: A Glider Pilot's Story."

THE ANCHOR MAN AND THE SKIPPER

SEAMAN 1ST CLASS GENE OXLEY AND LIEUTENANT COIT HENDLEY, JR.

Coast Guard LCI (L) 85

Death was not something Gene Oxley thought much about, even as a flurry of German machine gun bullets were whizzing past him, and nearby explosions from artillery shells were showering him with seawater. Getting killed was what happened to other guys, not him.

He hoped.

Whether driven by youthful bravado or a lucky feeling, the 20-year-old former Boy Scout had volunteered for the most dangerous job for any of the 30 crewmen of LCI (L) 85, a large infantry landing craft. The vessel, which was transporting 220 soldiers and navy personnel, was heading straight toward a section of Omaha Beach in the face of withering enemy fire.

All on board could hear and feel the scraping and banging of the hull against underwater obstacles that the Germans had planted to thwart the invaders. Oxley knew that any one of those obstructions—buried upright poles and three steel bars welded together to form "hedgehogs"—could be topped with plate-shaped Teller mines (named after the German word for "plate"). He wondered if his ship would hit one. He found out seconds later.

About 70 yards from shore, the 85 grounded onto a sand-bar—one that had been mined. A loud blast shook the landing craft and ripped a hole near the bow (front). No matter. This was where the troops would have to disembark. But first, Oxley would have to carry out his perilous task.

Hauling a long, sturdy line known as a "man rope" that was attached to a small 20-pound anchor, Oxley scampered down a skinny ramp that had been deployed off the port (left) side and jumped into the chest-high water. As the first person off the ship, he had to make it to shore and plant the anchor to secure the man rope so the troops could cling to this lifeline as they waded to the beach. They were carrying up to 100 pounds of gear and he knew that, without a man rope, men like them had drowned in previous invasions when they slipped below the surface and couldn't get up because of all the weight on their backs. *That's not going to happen this time*, he vowed to himself.

Ignoring the bullets splashing around him, Oxley trudged in the water, battled powerful currents, sidestepped mined obstacles, and fought through the heavy surf to reach the beach. But before he could set the anchor in the sand, bullets shot it out of his hands and snapped off the end of the line. Without wasting a second, he wrapped the loose end of the rope around his body several times and, leaning at a 45-degree angle with his back to the blazing enemy guns, he strained to keep the line taut. He was now a human anchor—fully exposed and completely defenseless.

He made for an easy target and a hard death.

Whatever fear he felt—and he felt plenty—was overshadowed by his determination to do his job. He possessed confidence in himself and a strong belief in luck, which was why he had volunteered three times for the same assignment the previous year when the 85 and its coast guard flotilla had invaded the beaches of Sicily and Salerno, Italy. He twice had jumped into the water and carried a man rope to the beach under enemy fire to help troops in their successful missions. For his bravery there, he earned a commendation combat medal.

Charging through the surf came naturally to Oxley because he was a strong swimmer. While attending Stilesville (Indiana) High School, where he had starred in baseball, basketball, and football, he had won several ribbons at swim meets and worked as a lifeguard at a YMCA summer camp. After graduation, he had enlisted in the coast guard. Six months later, the lanky red-haired teenager had been assigned to overseas duty on LCI (L) 85.

Skippered by 23-year-old Lieutenant (junior grade) Coit Hendley, Jr., the 158-foot-long vessel was specially designed so she could glide up to a beach in less than three feet of water. On D-Day, the 85 was carrying members of a beach battalion who were to organize the massive amounts of men, equipment, vehicles, and cargo that would be coming ashore during the invasion.

Circling in a staging area 10 miles from shore, the 85, which was part of the coast guard's 24-ship Flotilla 10, waited for its scheduled time to land on the far-right flank of sector Easy Red of Omaha Beach at H+2, or 8:30 a.m., two hours after the start of the invasion. The first eight assault battalions had already reached shore, and the next group, including 14 demolition teams, had landed two minutes later. They had only 30 minutes to blow up the exposed obstacles to clear pathways for thousands of landing craft like the 85. However, intense enemy fire had wiped out two demo teams and inflicted heavy casualties on the other teams. The survivors managed to blow five channels clear, but the tide rose too quickly to mark the lanes. By 8 a.m., the water had covered the remaining obstacles.

In the morning light, while the 85 waited for the signal to head for the beach, Oxley noticed that the men in the boat all wore grim expressions. When he gazed out toward the open water, he saw flashes from the guns of Allied warships that were shelling the coast. Perhaps it was his optimistic nature, but Oxley figured the invasion would be a piece of cake. *Oh, sure, the Krauts will put up a big fight, but we should easily beat them,* he thought as he threaded his way through the packed troops toward the bow. That wasn't the best place to be because the waves from the churning sea were crashing over the gunwales (the upper edge of the boat's side), drenching Oxley and others.

Finally, the control vessel for Easy Red hailed the 85 and directed Hendley to head in. One of the instruction manuals given to the crewmen during training noted that "hedgehogs and steel stakes will not prevent your beaching provided you go flat out. Your craft will crunch over them, bend them, and squash them into the sand with acceptable damage to your outer bottom. So drive on."

Standing on the vessel's bridge, Hendley picked out what he thought was a good spot to land and ordered his vessel full steam ahead. The ship plowed through many of the underwater obstacles as if they were made of plywood, prompting Oxley to think, *The manual was right.*

But as the 85 neared the beach, he saw troubling signs. Several smaller boats were drifting out of control, abandoned, shot to pieces, or hung up on mined obstacles. Heavy smoke shrouded the entire shoreline. Corpses, backpacks, and empty life belts were floating in the waves. He was beginning to believe that maybe he had been too optimistic.

The cliffs overlooking the beach seemed menacing to Oxley. When the 85 closed to within a few hundred yards of the beach, the Germans opened fire with machine guns, mortars, and artillery. Bullets struck the sides with metallic pings, and columns of water shot into the air from mortar rounds. "We're gonna catch hell," muttered a shipmate.

Oxley nodded. Concentrated machine gun fire was pinning down troops on the beach. Enemy 88mm artillery shells—the dreaded 88s—were finding their mark, blasting landing craft into oblivion. The wrecks and debris and the constant flow of boats bringing in more assault troops had created a huge traffic jam.

Four tanks were on the sand directly in front of the 85. Three of them were burning, but the fourth, which also had been hit, was still shooting. A line of soldiers who were stretched out on their bellies behind the shingle were firing at the German pillboxes and positions in and above the cliffs.

After seeing the water boiling with bullet strikes from hidden shore emplacements, a soldier on board the 85 let out a low whistle and said, "It looks like a mud puddle in a hailstorm. How will we make it to shore without getting shot to death?"

Oxley had no answer; he'd leave it up to fate. He was ready to carry the man rope and small anchor as soon as the 85 came to a halt. When it did, about 100 yards offshore, crewmen lowered the ramp. Oxley sprinted down and jumped in—and disappeared under the surface. Having already been soaked by the spray from the waves, the cold water didn't shock him. But finding himself 10 feet below the surface was a real problem, especially while holding a heavy line and 20-pound anchor.

As he struggled under the surf, his shipmates pulled him up with the rope and onto the ramp. Once he caught his breath, Oxley learned that the ship wasn't grounded on a sandbar but was hung up on a steel stake in much deeper water than anyone thought. There was no way to offload the troops from that spot. After the ramp was raised, the 85 backed off the obstruction and moved farther away from the beach while Hendley planned another approach.

Suddenly, a high-caliber artillery shell hit the 85 amidships (in the middle) and exploded in the number 3 troop compartment. Hendley could hear the screams of the beach battalion troops belowdecks as smoke poured out of the ventilation system. The medics who had accompanied the troops immediately began tending to the wounded, but the skipper could tell that the blast had killed many.

Hendley navigated the ship parallel to the beach for about 100 yards until he spotted an area that seemed clear of most of the debris. The 85 turned and sped toward shore until she went aground. As the bow hit the sand, however, she struck a mine that detonated under the hull, splitting a forward compartment.

Germans from a nearby pillbox concentrated their fire on the vessel's starboard (right) side, so the crew deployed the ramp on the port side only. That's when Oxley jumped into the water for the second time. Although it was deeper than what he had hoped—it reached his chest—he battled the strong currents and brought the small anchor and man rope to shore only to have the anchor shot out of his hands.

Now, as he braced himself on the beach with the line wrapped around him, he knew he was a perfect target. *Machine gun bullets are dropping around me like rain*, he thought. But he kept the line tight.

Several soldiers from another unit that had reached the beach earlier stopped shooting and sprinted over to help Oxley steady the line. Offshore, a bazooka-wielding GI who had jumped off the landing craft now stood in the water under the bow and fired at the pillbox while the troops on the 85 charged down the ramp.

At the same time, the German shore batteries zeroed in on the landing craft and began pummeling her. A shell struck the ramp, badly damaging it and knocking three soldiers into the drink. The 85's executive officer, Lieutenant (junior grade) Arthur Farrar, had been at the bottom of the ramp helping the soldiers disembark when the shell made a basketball-size hole in the hull after first grazing his left thigh and causing a large flesh wound.

With the damaged ramp dangling straight down, Farrar held on to it with one hand while using the other to grasp one of the soldiers, who was unconscious. Farrar kept the wounded man's head above the water, but he couldn't help the other two. One of them was able to grip the ramp to keep from drowning but their comrade lay floating facedown, lifeless. Crewmen eventually hauled them back onto the deck, including the dead soldier.

More explosions ripped into the 85, triggering fires and killing more troops. One shell crashed into the wheelhouse, where Chief Quartermaster Charles McWhirter was at the helm. The blast blew off his clothes, yet, incredibly, left him with only a small scratch on his back.

Because they couldn't use either ramp and casualties were piling up on the deck, soldiers began jumping over the side of the vessel trying to get to shore. Clutching the man rope that Oxley was holding, they began pulling themselves toward the shore through machine gun fire. While some had their rifles strapped to their shoulders, others held their weapons over their heads with one hand as they strained to reach shore. But it was slow going—and deadly.

"Come on!" Oxley yelled above the noise. "Come on! You can make it!" One dozen, two dozen, three dozen men leaped into the surf. He kept encouraging them, even though snipers and enemy gunners on the cliffs were targeting them. Every few seconds, one of the soldiers was struck and slipped under the water only to bob to the bloody surface moments later, dead.

His heart aching as much as his arms, Oxley cringed as, one by one, the soldiers were picked off. Seeing the Germans firing down at the Americans, he thought, *It's like shooting fish in a barrel.* Just 6 of the 36 men managed to make it to shore. The lifeline had turned into a death line. How or why none of the bullets had struck him yet, Oxley had no explanation. Nor did he want to think about it, although he was fully aware that luck has its limits.

After he noticed that no more troops were jumping off the 85—Hendley had halted the unloading—Oxley let go of the rope and flattened himself on the sand with the six troops. They tried to move forward, but each time a soldier stood up to advance, he was cut down. Having lost his shoes—the wet sand had sucked them off his feet—and his helmet, Oxley furiously dug a foxhole on the beach with his bare hands and balled up to make himself a smaller target. He had no weapon to defend himself.

Meanwhile, Hendley was trying to save his crippled ship and backed her off the sandbar. When Oxley saw the smoking, listing 85 moving away, he thought, *They're leaving without me!* He crawled out of the foxhole, sprang to his feet, and dashed near the water's edge, hoping to swim to the ship. But the Germans fired at him, forcing him to jump into another foxhole that someone else had dug.

When the 85 was out of range of the shore batteries, crewmen gave Hendley the bitter news: 15 were dead and 30 wounded. The landing craft had been hit 25 times by artillery shells. Bunks and blankets were on fire in troop compartments 1 and 2, and oil from a punctured fuel tank was burning in compartment 3. Water was streaming in from shell holes below the waterline and from the gash made by the mine.

The only good news was that none of the shells had destroyed the engine room, so the 85 was still operable. While the damage-control party worked to snuff out the blazes, which it did within 30 minutes, coast guard pharmacist's mates and army and navy doctors who were on board treated the wounded. Small boats came alongside the stricken craft and took off the remaining able-bodied troops and brought them to shore to face the same fierce onslaught that had wounded and killed their buddies on the ship.

The 85 continued to list from all the breaches in the hull while crewmembers manned pumps to keep it afloat. Not knowing if his sinking vessel could be saved, Hendley decided to get the wounded to a hospital ship as fast as possible, which, given the bad shape of his boat, turned out to be agonizingly slow.

Back on shore, Oxley was forced to move farther up the beach because the rising tide had flooded him out of his foxhole. He dug another one but soon had to abandon it. Over the next hour, the tide had washed him out of five such holes as the beach shrank until it was only 15 feet from the waterline to the base of a cliff.

I've got to find a way off this beach, Oxley told himself. Then he spotted a small landing craft that had come ashore about 100 yards away and was unloading troops. *Here's my chance.* As bullets kicked sand in his face, the sprinting Coastie reached the vessel seconds before it began backing off.

Once the boat was clear of the beach, one of her gunners turned his 20mm weapon on a pillbox on a nearby slope. It returned fire, which ignited a blaze on board. Moments later, an artillery shell landed smack in the middle of the deck, exploded, and split the vessel in half.

As the blast blew Oxley against a bulwark, he shielded his head with his hands. When he withdrew them from his face, he saw he was covered with blood and assumed he was wounded. It wasn't his blood, however, but that of a dead crewman next to him. Oxley then jumped off the stern (rear) of the craft, which sank in less than three minutes.

Once again, he swam, waded, and trudged to shore, where he dug another foxhole and wondered how much longer his luck would hold out. Not only was he still alive, he was still unhurt.

He soon spotted a large infantry landing craft, LCI (L) 93, beach herself a few yards off the shoreline. Ducking, crawling, and wading, he worked his way toward her. After unloading troops, the crew began trying to evacuate the wounded from the beach. But most of the litter bearers were being mowed down by enemy fire before they left the ramp.

Still counting on his good luck, Oxley helped the surviving crew bring the wounded onto the ship. When the last of the injured was aboard, he hopped onto the deck and became the newest—if temporary—member of the crew. *I'm safe at last*, he thought.

Unlike so many other landing craft, the 93 had unloaded troops without being hit by artillery because she had landed in an area where heavy smoke from several burning ships provided cover. Now Lieutenant (junior grade) Budd Bornhoft, commander of the vessel, announced to the crew that the 93 was returning to the transport area to collect another load of soldiers and ferry them to the embattled beach.

After picking up nearly 200 troops, the landing craft was nearing the shore when Oxley told a crewman, "I've already survived two sinking ships. I hope I'm not a jinx for you guys."

The 93 landed so close to the beach there was no need for a man rope and quickly unloaded the soldiers without attracting the enemy. Before the ship could push off, 16 crewmen from LCI (L) 487, which was burning several hundred yards away on the beach, rushed aboard.

That caught the attention of the German artillerymen who had been firing at the 487. Now they trained their big guns on the 93 and scored several direct hits that killed 1 and wounded 11. The survivors—including Oxley—were forced to abandon the landing craft, slog their way to shore, dig foxholes, and helplessly watch the vessel burn to the waterline.

So, for the third time that day, Oxley was curled up in a hand-dug pit in the sand in the deadly Easy Red sector of the Normandy coast. There was no doubt in Oxley's mind that he, indeed, was a jinx. Still, no enemy bullet had touched him. As he lay in the sand, he wondered about the fate of his shipmates on the 85.

He would later learn that they had slowly coaxed the craft to the transport area and tied up next to the USS *Samuel Chase*, which took aboard the wounded, including four crewmen, and the dead. The 85's crew continued to pump water out of the flooded compartments, but the water was coming in too fast, and the vessel continued to list. The salvage tug AT 98 came alongside to help with more pumps, but it was no use.

On orders from Hendley, the crew abandoned ship and scrambled aboard the tug. At 2:30 p.m., the 85 capsized, exposing the bottom of her battered hull, which now threatened to become a navigation hazard to hundreds of Allied ships in the area. As a result, members from a salvage boat put a demolition charge in the 85's stern and exploded it. The landing craft, which had served so gallantly in previous invasions of hostile shores without enduring any serious damage, sank 14 fathoms (84 feet) to the bottom. Before it was sunk, Hendley had put the 85's confidential material in a weighted sack so it would go down with the ship.

His glum crew huddled together on the deck of the tug, but Hendley sat away from them. He wanted to be alone. *I'm to blame for the deaths and wounding of all those men,* he told himself. Overcome by a heavy feeling of guilt, he wept. He would later write in his official After Action Report, "The 88's began hitting the ship, they tore into the compartments, and exploded on the exposed deck. Machine guns opened up. Men were hit and men were mutilated. There was no such thing as a minor wound."

Back on shore, Oxley, who still had no weapon, remained hunkered down for several hours in his hole as the fighting raged on. Every time he looked up, he counted more dead and dying in the sand. By early evening, the intensity had eased. The steady stream of Americans had worn down the German resistance.

Oxley scrambled out of his foxhole and began helping evacuate the wounded to a landing craft that had just offloaded soldiers and navy personnel. A destroyer, the USS *Doyle*, came close to shore and blasted the beach defenses while also sending out small boats to transport the wounded from the beach. Although he could have climbed into any one of the vessels, Oxley waited until the last one. When he arrived aboard the *Doyle*, the cold, wet, hungry seaman could barely stand because he was so exhausted.

A corpsman who checked him over shook his head in disbelief because he couldn't find any bullet or shrapnel wounds on Oxley. "Are you sure you weren't shot somewhere?" the corpsman asked.

"I'm sure, why?" the seaman asked.

"Because a piece of shrapnel tore out the seat of your pants."

Oxley twisted around and saw, for the first time, that indeed the rear of his pants was missing, exposing his skivvies. He had no idea when or exactly where that happened during his 10-hour ordeal. "I don't know why I didn't get hit because the Germans were machine-gunning us all over the place," he said. "I just dug my heels in the sand and prayed. At first, I didn't have time to be scared. Then I got pretty scared, but I guess that's natural. And now that my day is over, I'm shaking like a leaf."

When Oxley returned to his port in Dartmouth, England, three days later, he walked into the barracks and shocked his fellow Coasties, who tumbled out of their beds and happily slapped him on the back and shook his hand. "We all thought you were dead," one of them said.

"Nah," Oxley replied. "Just lucky. Why, I'm the luckiest boy of D-Day!"

Oxley also was awarded the Silver Star—the military's third-highest combat medal—for his gallantry on D-Day. His commendation cited his "extraordinary courage in volunteering and twice taking a line ashore, in the face of heavy machine gun and shell fire in order to assist troops unloading from the ship to the beach through chest-deep water."

In 1981, the town of Milford, Ohio, where he settled long after the war, honored Oxley by naming a park after him. Shortly before the dedication, he told the Cincinnati Enquirer, "I'm not a hero and I don't pretend to be." He added that memories of D-Day still haunted him. "I wake up at night at least once a week with sweat pouring all over me. I go over every detail of the whole thing." Oxley, who suffered four heart attacks, died in 1992 at the age of 68.

LCI (L) 85 earned four battle stars in World War II, and, like all the landing craft of Flotilla 10, was also awarded the Coast Guard Unit Commendation for her service during the invasion of Normandy.

Although Lieutenant Hendley felt guilty over the loss of his ship, the coast guard awarded him the Silver Star for his actions. The commendation accompanying the medal said, "Hendley successfully landed his troops despite the mining of his vessel, fire in three compartments, and concentration of enemy fire while unloading. His courage and seamanship in directing repairs and retracting from the beach resulted in saving the lives of many wounded aboard."

After the war, Hendley spent 25 years as a newspaper reporter and then as an editor of the Washington Star *before becoming managing editor of the* Washington Times. *He and his wife, Barbara, raised four children. He died in 1985 at age 64.*

THE SMOKING GUNS

1ST SERGEANT LEONARD "BUD" LOMELL AND STAFF SERGEANT JACK KUHN

2nd Platoon, D Company, 2nd Ranger Battalion

It was nothing short of a suicide mission.

Two hundred and twenty-five Rangers—the army's most elite fighting men—were charged with a seemingly impossible assignment: They had to climb an imposing 100-foot-tall cliff in daylight while the Germans above fired down on them. Those Rangers who somehow made it to the top would then have to fight their way past the enemy, which far outnumbered them, and destroy a battery of six powerful 155mm long-range guns.

If the Rangers failed, the weapons, which had plenty of ammunition, were in position to fire their huge shells up to 12 miles away and deliver unspeakable horror, destroying countless Allied ships and killing thousands of troops storming Omaha and Utah Beaches.

The Rangers' main objective was Pointe-du-Hoc, a three-sided cliff that jutted out from the Normandy coast into the English Channel. Toward the back of this outcropping, the Germans had strategically placed the huge weapons in heavily reinforced concrete bunkers. The enemy also had constructed an elaborate, well-protected outpost on the edge of the cliff, giving an unobstructed view to spotters who could call in coordinates to the gunners of the 155s farther inland.

The fate of D-Day hinged on the Rangers' accomplishing their mission. They had to silence those guns.

For the crossing of the English Channel on the night of June 5, the Rangers sailed in the massive Allied armada aboard the SS *Nieuw Amsterdam*, a Dutch ocean liner that had been converted into a troop ship. 1st Sergeant Leonard "Bud" Lomell, 24, of 2nd Platoon, D Company, 2nd Ranger Battalion, felt lucky that he and his comrades each had their own private rooms to relax in before the invasion.

He took some time to write a note to his Scandinavian immigrant parents, George and Pauline Lomell, who had adopted him as an infant in Brooklyn and raised him in Point Pleasant Beach, New Jersey. He thanked them for instilling in him a strong work ethic that led to an athletic scholarship at Tennessee Wesleyan College, where he became editor of the school newspaper and president of his fraternity. As he had reminded his parents earlier when he joined the army shortly after graduation and again after he volunteered for the Rangers, he felt duty-bound to serve his country.

Lomell didn't have any trouble catching a few hours of sleep while the liner sailed toward Normandy. His mindset was that of a typical Ranger: confident and optimistic. Willing to try the impossible, they had trained hard for two years under extreme conditions in the US and England. They had scaled mountains in full battle gear, swam in rough surf, run obstacle courses in record times, received detailed intelligence training, and sharpened survival skills until they had molded themselves into the army's best of the best. They were ready.

At 4 a.m. on June 6, when they were 12 miles off the Normandy coast, the Rangers of Force A—consisting of D, E, and F Companies—left the ocean liner and hopped into 10 small assault landing crafts known as LCAs, which were manned by British sailors. Accompanying them were two supply boats and four DUKW amphibious trucks (boats that can drive on land), nicknamed Ducks.

As the Rangers headed toward the coast in heavy seas, some began throwing up from seasickness. Others watched in awe as Allied planes completed the final phase of their bombardment of Pointe-du-Hoc, which had been going on for days. Then the battleship USS *Texas* took over, shelling the top of the cliff for the next hour.

Viewing the orange explosions in the predawn darkness from the bow of LCA 668, Lomell told Staff Sergeant Jack Kuhn, 24, "I feel like a country boy at the county fair watching fireworks."

"Pretty exciting," Kuhn replied.

As their bobbing LCA moved closer to the beach, the waves were breaking over the sides, soaking the Rangers. Because the boat's pumps couldn't handle all the water sloshing around inside, the men had to bail with their helmets to keep the craft from sinking.

Another LCA, this one carrying D Company's commanding officer, Captain Duke Slater, and 20 men, was swamped, leaving them treading water for more than an hour before they were picked up by a rescue ship. "Give us some dry clothes, weapons, and ammunition," Slater told the skipper, "and get us back to the Pointe!" But the ship's physician ordered them to return to England because they were suffering from hypothermia—loss of body heat—from their lengthy exposure in the numbing 50-degree water.

One of the Rangers' two supply boats, which was hauling ammunition, sank in the stormy sea. The other one avoided a similar fate only after the men dumped more than half her load to stay afloat.

At daybreak, around 6:30 a.m., the *Texas* stopped her shelling in anticipation of the Rangers' assault. When their LCAs came within 300 yards of the beach, Lomell pointed to the cliff, shook his head, and told Kuhn, "Something's not right. That doesn't look anything like the Pointe-du-Hoc in the photos that I studied."

Meanwhile, in the lead boat, Lieutenant Colonel James Rudder, commander of the Rangers, realized they were heading toward the wrong cliff. The rolling seas, wind, and current as well as poor navigation had shoved the LCAs off course toward Pointe-de-la-Percée. After ordering the British coxswain to turn west and go parallel to the shore toward Pointe-du-Hoc, Rudder signaled to his small flotilla to follow him.

"We're nearly three miles from our objective," Lomell told

his men. "This will put us about thirty minutes behind schedule. That's not good."

The delay allowed the Germans, who had taken cover during the bombing and shelling, to regroup. They emerged from their bunkers and began firing at the Rangers from atop the cliffs with machine guns, rifles, mortars, and even bigger guns, one of which shelled and sank a Duck. In Lomell's LCA, Rangers were still bailing water while dodging bullets and vomiting at the same time.

To help the Rangers, two destroyers, the USS *Satterlee* and HMS *Talybont*, fired at the Germans, trying, with some success, to drive them back from the edge of the cliff. Shortly after 7 a.m., Force A arrived several yards off the narrow, stony beach below Pointe-du-Hoc. Waiting for the ramp to go down, Lomell decided to repeat to his men what his football coach back at Point Pleasant Beach High School said before every game. "Charge hard, low, and fast," Lomell, who was leader of the 2nd Platoon, told his comrades. "We must stay together as a team. Now, let's go get 'em!"

When the ramp of the LCA dropped, Lomell—the first one off—took one step and then felt a sharp pain on his right side just above the hip. A bullet had gone right through him from front to back without hitting any bones or organs.

The impact spun him around, and he lost his balance. Lomell toppled off the ramp into an underwater bomb crater, plunging to the bottom several feet below the surface. He tried to get up but couldn't because he was too loaded down with his assault vest, gas mask, ammunition, helmet, grenades, sub-machine gun, pistol, and rope. He was also holding a rocket launcher. Without panicking, he thought, *I've got to ditch my equipment*. But before he did, two of his platoon buddies pulled him up and dragged him to shore.

Relieved that he had suffered only a flesh wound, Lomell told himself, *Ignore the pain and get on with the mission*.

Using a modern version of an ancient military technique, the Rangers fired rocket-propelled anchor-like devices called grapnels that were attached to ropes and rope ladders. The men were hoping the grapnels would reach the top of the cliff and dig into the ground so they could climb the ropes. Unfortunately, many of the ropes were waterlogged from ocean spray, making them too heavy to reach that high, so they fell short. Still, enough grapnels did snag the ground at the top for the Rangers to ascend.

But reaching the ropes proved deadly. As the Rangers sprinted off the LCAs, they were peppered with enemy fire from both flanks and above. In the first few minutes of this assault, a German machine gun from the left side killed or wounded 15 Rangers.

The earlier Allied bombing and shelling at the top of Pointe-du-Hoc had dislodged huge chunks of the clay soil, which slid down onto the rocks at the base of the cliff. Although the fallen dirt provided the Rangers with a 20-foot earthen ramp, rain and mud had made the cliff face more slippery than anticipated.

As Rangers began pulling themselves up hand over hand, the Germans above leaned over the side, fired at them, dropped grenades, and cut ropes, sending several men plummeting to their deaths. Other Rangers tried climbing using only their hands and feet rather than ropes. Some of the men delayed their ascents so they could provide cover fire from the beach. The first Americans who made it to the top then fired their tommy guns—the nickname for a Thompson submachine gun—and tried to push the enemy away from the edge to give their comrades below a better chance of joining them.

Sergeant William "L-Rod" Petty had climbed 40 feet when he began a slow fall while still holding on to the rope. At first he thought the Germans had cut it, but then he realized that the grappling hook was slipping through the ground on top.

As Petty continued his slow drop, Sergeant Billy McHugh, who was climbing a rope ladder a few feet away from him, shouted, "Hey, L-Rod, you're going the wrong way! You're supposed to be going up like me."

"Comic," Petty growled. After he landed at the bottom, he used a different rope. It took him three tries before he could reach the top.

Lomell looked up at the cliff and thought, *Can enough of us make it to the top and complete the mission? If we can, we'll win. We always do.* Like all Rangers, he refused to let fear slow him down. *Heck, I've already been shot, and I'm still standing.*

As bullets flew, he, Kuhn, and the rest of the platoon tore across the beach and reached for the ropes, which were slick from mud, sweat, and blood. The muscular 5-foot, 9-inch Lomell had rope-climbed vertical walls tougher than this, but not under these conditions. Each yard up the rope was harder than the one before. As he neared the top, his arm and leg muscles were quivering and burning worse than he had ever felt before.

On the rope next to him, Sergeant Robert Fruling, the platoon's radioman who was carrying on his back a large radio with a tall antenna, was struggling, too. Just short of the top, Fruling gasped, "Bud, help me! Help me! I'm losing my strength." He reached out with a shaky hand but Lomell wouldn't grab it, telling him, "Hold on, Bob! It's taking everything I've got to get this far. I can't help you."

Above Fruling on the same rope was Sergeant Leonard Rubin, a born athlete and one of the platoon's strongest men. "Rubin!" shouted Lomell. "Help Bob! I don't think he can make it."

While clutching the rope with one hand, Rubin reached down with the other, gripped Fruling by the back of the neck, and held him to give him a breather. Then, after reaching the top, Rubin helped him up. When the sapped Fruling tried to stand, he wobbled.

Directly below and still climbing, Lomell looked up and saw the radio's antenna whipping back and forth. *If he's shot, he's going to fall right on top of me, and we'll both plunge to our deaths*, Lomell thought. "Bob, get down!" Lomell yelled. "Get down! You're gonna draw fire on us!" Just then a bullet grazed

Fruling's helmet, stunning him and knocking him to the ground. Another bullet slammed into the radio that he had just lugged to the top, destroying it.

After climbing the cliff, Lomell scrambled into a shell hole to catch his breath. In a crater next to him, Private Ralph Davis, a Tennessee country boy who was one of the Rangers' best sharpshooters, dropped his pants and went to the bathroom. "Hey," he told those around him, "when you gotta go, you gotta go."

Lomell scanned the landscape and noticed it didn't look anything like the photos, maps, and sketches he had studied. The bombardment had turned the top of Pointe-du-Hoc into a bleak scene that resembled the surface of the moon. Hundreds of craters, some as wide as 30 feet and as deep as 6 feet, covered the area. Any landmarks such as houses and small groups of trees, called copses, had been flattened. Bombs also had smashed enemy gun casements and left them scattered in huge chunks of concrete bigger than army tanks. *They look like a giant's toy blocks*, Lomell thought.

The craters were a blessing to the Rangers because they provided plenty of cover. Within 15 minutes of landing, most of the men of Force A had reached the top and were hopping from one crater to the next, firing at the German defenders.

Each platoon had a specific mission. F Company: Destroy guns 1 and 2 as well as the antiaircraft gun positioned on the eastern sector of the cliff top. E Company: Take out the coastal observation post and gun 3. Lomell's D Company: Disable guns 4, 5, and 6 on the western point of Pointe-du-Hoc.

Lomell and his men began fighting their way toward their objective, trying to avoid lengthy firefights. In one crater, Lomell found Captain Gilbert Baugh, E Company's commanding officer, in shock and bleeding badly after a bullet went through the back of his hand and into the magazine of the .45-caliber Colt pistol he was still gripping, although barely. Lomell gave him an injection of the drug morphine to dull the pain and told him, "There's nothing more I can do for you. We gotta keep moving, Captain. We'll send a medic to you, so just stay put. You're gonna be all right."

With bayonets fixed on their weapons, Lomell led his platoon to another crater. Ready to advance, Sergeant Morris Webb and Corporal Robert Carty were in a line right behind him. The moment the three emerged, the Germans opened fire, forcing them to jump back into the crater for cover. Webb screamed in pain after he backpedaled right onto Carty's bayonet and was accidentally stabbed in his thigh. Lomell injected Webb with morphine and said, "You'll have to stay here alone, Webb. We can't waste any more time 'cause we gotta keep moving. If we see a medic, we'll send him to you. Good luck."

The Germans were putting up stiff resistance, shooting from trenches and machine gun nests in the fortified area. The Rangers moved through minefields and under barbed wire fences, dealing with sniper fire as well as shelling from powerful 88mm guns. One by one, 10 of Lomell's men fell dead or wounded, but he and the remaining half of his platoon kept advancing until they finally reached their objective—only to face a terrible surprise. The fearsome guns that they had fought so hard to reach, the ones that showed up so clearly on the most recent aerial reconnaissance photos, were nothing more than telephone poles painted gray in casements 4, 5, and 6.

"I don't believe this!" Lomell snarled. "What happened here?"

"You mean to tell me that we battled all this way and took all those casualties for this?" Kuhn griped.

Men from the other platoons encountered the same disheartening shock at casements 1, 2, and 3. The Germans had faked out the Americans.

"All this blood and sweat for nothing!" snapped Kuhn, spitting in disgust. "There were never any guns here!"

"Oh, they were here," Lomell corrected him. "The Germans just moved them. The question is where." Gritting his teeth in frustration, he told his men, "No sense cryin' about it. We need to get to our next objective." Like the two other platoons, 2nd Platoon began moving inland and westward toward a critical intersection on a paved coastal road that connected the town of Grandcamp-Maisy with Vierville-sur-Mer. The Rangers needed to set up a roadblock at the intersection, which was near Grandcamp, to prevent German reinforcements from reaching Omaha and Utah Beaches a few miles away. E and F Companies were also setting up roadblocks at other points on the highway. In addition, the Americans were to search for and cut all enemy communication wires running alongside the road.

Lomell, Kuhn, and platoon scout Private Jack Conovoy were crossing a road when an enemy sniper opened up. Lomell and Kuhn made it safely to the other side, diving into a hedgerow. But Conovoy lay flat on his face on the road. "I'm hit!" he yelped. "I'm hit!"

"Do you need me to come get you?" Lomell asked from behind a thicket.

"No, I can crawl to you." While Lomell and Kuhn provided cover fire, Conovoy slinked over to them.

"Where are you shot?" Lomell asked.

Conovoy pulled down his pants and pointed to his rear end. "Right in the butt."

Stifling a laugh, Lomell said, "The bullet went through one cheek and almost through the other one. I can actually see the bullet. It's barely sticking out."

"Well, pull it out, but don't throw it away," Conovoy said. "I want to save it as a souvenir."

With his fingers, Lomell yanked out the bullet and handed it to Conovoy. Kuhn then poured sulfa powder—a first aid treatment to reduce the risk of infection—into the wounds in the private's rear end. Conovoy pulled up his pants and the three continued westward with the rest of the platoon.

When they reached the intersection, Lomell learned from Lieutenant George Kerchner, D Company's acting commanding officer, that only 20 men out of the 70 from the company were still able to fight. The rest were dead or wounded. Even so, D Company had advanced faster and farther into enemy territory than the other Ranger companies of Force A.

By 8 a.m.—less than an hour after storming the beach at Pointe-du-Hoc—D Company established a roadblock designed to thwart any German reinforcements from using the highway. Meanwhile, Lomell and Kuhn headed up the road in search of a good observation point that would let them see any advancing enemy soldiers from far away.

"You know, Jack, those 155s are around here someplace," Lomell said. "The Germans probably moved them off the Pointe two weeks ago when we began bombing it. There have to be some telltale signs of where the guns are now."

"They're too big to have been towed by jeeps," Kuhn said. "It would take heavy trucks to pull them."

"Which means they would leave tracks in a dirt road," Lomell added. "Let's see if we can find any that would lead us to the guns."

They soon noticed that low-hanging branches had been snapped off trees where a country lane, lined with a hedgerow on either side, met the highway at a T-intersection. "Big trucks could have broken the branches when they turned onto this secondary road," said Lomell. "And look at the tracks in the dirt."

"They belong to something heavy—something like the wheels on a 155," said Kuhn. "This road is wide enough for them to be towed."

"It's worth exploring," Lomell said.

Going at a quick pace, they leapfrogged down the lane. First, Lomell would run several feet forward while Kuhn covered him. Then Kuhn would hustle past Lomell while Lomell covered him. Every so often, they stopped and peered through the hedgerows, looking for the guns—and the enemy.

A few minutes into the search, Lomell peeked into an orchard and gasped. He turned to Kuhn and whispered, "Jack, we've found them! Here are those guns!"

Among the apple trees stood five 155mm guns, all camouflaged under netting covered with leaves to hide them from aerial reconnaissance. The guns, which had shells neatly stacked beside them at the ready, were set up in a battery with their 20-foot-long barrels angled skyward toward Utah Beach, which was well within their reach. There was no sign of the sixth 155.

Kuhn rushed over to Lomell, took in the scene, and said, "I can't believe there are no gun crews manning them or at least guarding them."

Lomell pointed to an area next to a farmhouse about 100 yards away from them where a German officer was talking to an estimated 75 soldiers. "There are the gun crews," he said. "It looks like they're preparing to man their guns, although they don't seem to be in any hurry."

"They're hindered right now," said Kuhn. "I bet they don't have any firing orders because we've cut their communications, and E Company killed their spotters at the observation post at the Pointe first thing." Both men knew that until the Germans could drive off the Rangers and install new spotters on the coast, the gunners couldn't fire the 155s with much accuracy.

"They're acting like they don't have a clue that the Rangers are this close to them," said Lomell. "None of them expected us to make it this far inland so fast. I can't believe our luck. No good artilleryman would leave his gun unattended like this. Jack, here's our chance to take out these guns. Give me your thermite grenade and cover me."

Kuhn handed over his thermite grenade, a powerful incendiary device that produced intense heat from a chemical reaction and burned through most anything it touched, including steel. It made little noise or smoke. Each Ranger had been issued such a grenade.

"If one of the Germans even looks my way or starts walking toward the guns, I want you to shoot him," Lomell said. "That'll clue me to leave, and we'll run back to the platoon."

Kuhn hid in a secluded spot in the hedgerow to cover Lomell, who moved toward the guns from the rear. Crawling along a heavily foliaged swale and remaining out of the line of sight by the oblivious Germans, Lomell thought, *I have only two grenades, but I have to damage all of the guns.* Worried that at any moment, a German would jump him or shoot him in the back, he crept up to the first gun and placed a thermite grenade into the traversing gears—they swiveled and raised and lowered the weapon—and pulled the pin. The grenade quickly burned and melted the gears, welding them together to make the gun inoperable. For added assurance that it wouldn't work, Lomell wrapped his field jacket around his tommy gun to muffle the sound as he smashed the 155's gunsight with the butt of his weapon. Still undetected by the Germans, he moved on to the second gun and jammed the other thermite grenade into the gears and ignited it. He then busted its gunsight as well as those on the other three 155s.

He scuttled back to Kuhn and said, "Jack, we gotta get more grenades."

The pair sprinted up the lane to the Ranger roadblock and collected more thermite grenades from their comrades. Then the two dashed back to their spot in the hedgerow to see if the Germans had discovered the sabotage. "Great," Lomell gloated. "They still don't know what we've done. Come on, let's put the other guns out of commission for good."

Lomell and Kuhn sneaked up on the battery. After Kuhn ignited another thermite grenade in the mechanism of the first gun for extra measure, he hid behind it and covered Lomell, who darted from gun to gun, lighting the grenades in the most vulnerable places. The extreme heat from the grenades began welding moving parts such as gears, cranks, hinges, and breechblocks until the weapons became inoperable.

While Lomell was wrecking the guns, Kuhn watched the glowing molten metal slither through the guns' mechanisms. *Oh, what a beautiful sight,* he thought. *Won't the Germans be surprised when they try to fire them!* He turned his attention back to the unsuspecting gun crews, aiming his weapon at them, ready to fire if necessary. *I have them right where I want them*. But then another thought crossed his mind: *They're bound to see what we're doing and come after us. If so, we'll be totally outnumbered. I have only three clips of ammo.*

"Hey, Bud, hurry up!" Kuhn whispered. "Let's get out of here!"

In less than 10 minutes, the two had disabled the entire five-gun battery. As they crawled to the other side of the hedgerow, a gigantic explosion violently shook the ground, lifted them in the air, and threw them onto the country lane. Lomell and Kuhn were showered with rocks, dirt, leaves, and debris. The blast was so loud that their ears kept ringing, making it hard to hear.

Scrambling to his feet, Kuhn said, "What was that?"

"I don't know," Lomell replied. "Run, just run!"

They returned to the roadblock and joined their comrades. It was nearing 9 a.m., just under two hours from the time they had landed. "We did it!" Lomell gloated.

He and Kuhn then learned the source of the explosion. At the same time the pair was immobilizing the five guns, a patrol led by Sergeant Frank Rupinski from E Company had discovered the sixth gun, which was hidden in another area of the orchard next to an unguarded ammunition dump and gunpowder storage area. After igniting a thermite grenade in the big gun, the Rangers used high-explosive charges to detonate the ammo and powder, which created the monster blast that knocked down Lomell and Kuhn.

"I don't mind getting tossed by an explosion like that," said

Lomell. "It means we successfully completed our main mission. We took out the guns of Pointe-du-Hoc."

The surviving Rangers couldn't enjoy their success on the Pointe because they had to fend off repeated attacks from the Germans for two and a half days. The Rangers were outmanned and low on food and ammo. Even though their numbers had dwindled to only 90 men still fit for combat from the original 225, they valiantly resisted until reinforcements finally arrived.

For his D-Day heroics, Lomell received the Distinguished Service Cross (the military's second-highest combat medal), the British Military Medal, and the French Legion of Honor. Wounded two more times during the war, he earned a battlefield commission to second lieutenant and later a Silver Star for his actions in the capture of Castle Hill in the Battle of the Hürtgen Forest, in Germany. In 1994, he was inducted into the Ranger Hall of Fame.

After the war, Lomell returned to New Jersey, where he enrolled at Rutgers University and earned a law degree in 1951. As founder and senior partner of the Lomell Law Firm, in Toms River, he practiced law until he was 78 years old. Throughout his career, he served as a director of numerous banks, companies, and nonprofit organizations. He and his wife, Charlotte, raised three daughters.

In 1999, the Borough of Point Pleasant Beach dedicated a monument to Lomell at Veterans Park. The monument features a replica of the grappling hook used by the Rangers at Pointe-du-Hoc as well as a plaque detailing his combat exploits.

He died in 2011 at home at the age of 91. The following year, Ocean County officials honored his memory by naming a newly created connector road Lomell Lane, at Garden State Parkway Exit 83.

For his D-Day efforts, Kuhn received a Silver Star and earned a second one in the Battle of Brest, where he was wounded. He later was inducted into the Ranger Hall of Fame. After a stint in the Marine Corps during the Korean War, Kuhn joined the Altoona (Pennsylvania) Police Department, where he worked his way up through the ranks to become chief of police. He retired from the force in 1976.

He died in 2002 at the age of 82. Two years later, the state legislature designated a section of State Route 4013 in Blair County as the Jack E. Kuhn Memorial Highway.

The 2nd Ranger Battalion received the Presidential Unit Citation for its bold efforts during the Normandy assault. In his oral history, Lieutenant James Eikner said, "Had we not been there [at Pointe-du-Hoc], we felt quite sure that those guns would have . . . brought much death and destruction down on our men on the beaches and our ships at sea. But . . . the big guns had been put out of commission, and the paved highway had been cut, and we had roadblocks denying its use to the enemy. So by 0900 [9 a.m.] our mission was accomplished. The Rangers at Pointe-du-Hoc were the first American forces on D-Day to accomplish their mission—and we are proud of that."

BLOODIED BUT UNBOWED

CORPORAL WAVERLY "WOODY" WOODSON, JR.
320th Barrage Balloon Battalion

Aboard an LCT—a large landing barge carrying several vehicles and more than 50 troops toward embattled Omaha Beach—army medic Woody Woodson gazed in sadness at the blood-and-oil-streaked water speckled with floating corpses.

His sorrow deepened as the LCT motored past several wounded men who were treading in the choppy sea and pleading for help after their boat had sunk. His vessel couldn't stop, not after an officer in a small launch nearby had yelled through a megaphone to the skipper, "You are not a rescue ship! Keep going and get onshore!"

Bullets began slamming into the hull, so some soldiers jumped into the jeeps onboard the LCT for added protection. Woodson ducked behind a truck filled with medical supplies.

When his boat was a few hundred yards offshore, the stern struck an underwater mine, producing a blast that knocked Woodson off his feet. The craft was still seaworthy, but the explosion had disabled the rudder and the engine. With no steering or power, the LCT drifted at the mercy of the wind, tide, and current, which were pushing it closer to the beach and within range of German batteries.

The aimless vessel then hit another mine on the starboard side, killing and wounding more than a dozen men. As it neared the shoreline, gunners on the ship's catwalk unleashed two 40mm weapons at the Germans, who returned fire with a vengeance. The LCT now became a favorite target of the enemy.

Before Woodson had a chance to help the wounded, a mortar round struck the ship near the stern, causing more fatalities. Looking up at the catwalk, he saw the gunners were dead, their bodies draped over a railing. Seconds later, another round landed on the hood of the jeep where the four soldiers earlier had sought safety inside. All four were incinerated along with others nearby.

Two more mortar rounds barely missed the crippled LCT. Next, a few feet away from Woodson, a round landed squarely on the steel deck and exploded in a blast that rattled his brain. Hot, razor-sharp shrapnel hurtled through the air and ripped into a soldier who had been standing next to him. The man died instantly.

Burning shards of metal struck Woodson, too. Knocked to the deck and dazed, he felt sharp, searing pains in his lower extremities. He reached down and touched his buttocks and upper right thigh. When he withdrew his hand, it was dripping with blood. Realizing that the shrapnel had sliced him open like a knife through a tenderloin steak, he thought, *I'm going to die.*

Raised in Philadelphia by loving parents who strongly believed in higher education, Woodson had dreams of becoming a doctor. Extremely bright and possessing a love of science, he attended Lincoln University in Pennsylvania. But the United States was at war. Rather than wait to be drafted, the 20-year-old African American premed student dropped out of school in 1942 during his sophomore year to enlist in the army because, he told his family, "I want to do my part to defeat the Nazis."

At the time, the US military was racially segregated, which mirrored the attitude of much of the country. The War Department generally assigned black servicemen to roles as cooks, stewards, supply clerks, or stevedores (dock workers) or put them into low-profile units in the rear. Only about nine percent of black troops in Europe were in combat units.

Although African Americans had few opportunities to become officers, Woodson tried anyway. He passed an exam weighted heavily in favor of whites to earn a slot in Anti-Aircraft Artillery Officer Candidate School. Woodson earned high marks, but the army claimed there were no positions open to him in the AAA corps—a story black men like him heard far too often. He was sent to Camp Tyson in northwest Tennessee for training as a medic for the 320th Barrage Balloon

Battalion, one of the army's four all–African American balloon units. Not surprisingly, these units were led by white officers.

Barrage balloons were designed to foil enemy planes by hovering over strategic sites. When inflated with hydrogen, these unmanned, blimp-like gasbags, which were bigger than school buses (up to 60 feet long and about 23 feet in diameter), floated several thousand feet high and were tethered to the ground with metal cables. When placed near each other in large numbers, they prevented strafing because low-flying planes risked striking one of the strong cables, which would shear off the wings. Many of the balloons also carried explosives to make a virtual airborne minefield.

The balloons forced enemy planes to fly higher, which was a plus for the Americans for two reasons: Planes at slightly greater altitude came within better range of antiaircraft artillery, which couldn't effectively hit low-flying ones. Secondly, the ability of enemy dive bombers to accurately hit targets on the ground was hindered when flying higher.

On his way to Camp Tyson, Woodson learned a bitter truth about life in the South. Although he had felt the stings of racial discrimination while growing up in Philadelphia, what he experienced after crossing the Mason-Dixon Line was far worse. Getting to Camp Tyson by train, he and his fellow African American enlistees and draftees were ordered to keep closed the curtains of the windows of their segregated blacks-only passenger cars. The curtains would cloak them from certain white bigots who lay in wait on trackside hills, hoping to shoot at the black passengers as the train passed by.

What shocked Woodson the most after he settled in at Camp Tyson was how much better German POWs were treated on American soil than were black US soldiers. Even though the prisoners were officially the enemy, thousands of them worked on Southern farms for pay in accordance to the rules of war created by the Geneva Convention. Many of these POWs—who were all white—were granted certain privileges for good behavior and were allowed to eat in the very same restaurants that refused to seat black men in uniform. Some of these establishments did allow African American troops to eat, but only if they took their meals outside. Like his comrades, Woodson fumed whenever he saw German prisoners share cigarettes and jokes with their white American guards and make friendly conversation with the townspeople.

As black recruits by the thousands continued to arrive at military bases throughout the South, racist locals went out of their way to make them feel unwelcome. In 1942, the Southern Governors Conference unanimously objected to the War Department sending any African American soldiers to the South for training. Alabama governor Frank Dixon publicly called it a "grave mistake."

At Camp Tyson, Woodson heard firsthand accounts of Northern-raised black troops who were dragged off Southern buses at gunpoint for refusing to sit in the back. Any white soldier who sided with his African American comrades was often kicked off, too. Paris, Tennessee, the nearest town to the camp, didn't have a single white-owned restaurant where blacks were allowed to eat inside.

Despite the racism, the overwhelming number of men of the 320th sang the praises of their white commanding officer, Lieutenant Colonel Leon Reed, a South Carolina–born career soldier who graduated high school when he was 15 and attended the famed military school The Citadel on a scholarship. He was fair and managed the men with the respect they deserved. The same couldn't be said for the second in command, Captain William "Wild Bill" Taylor, a Texan who referred to the soldiers to their face as "Boy" and often treated them harshly and with contempt.

Training was tough—25-mile hikes in the woods, predawn runs with 60-pound backpacks, endless calisthenics at all hours of the day and night, and obstacle-course tests under live fire. The recruits learned how to deploy balloons, shoot M1 rifles, handle grenades, and fight hand-to-hand. Much of Woodson's time at Camp Tyson was spent learning how to treat the wounded under battlefield conditions.

He and his comrades didn't know it at the time, but they were being trained for a special—and what would be an historic—mission. They would make up the only all-black combat unit to storm the shores of Normandy on D-Day.

Early in 1944, the 320th was shipped to the United Kingdom, where it underwent more training in Pontypool, in southwestern Wales, and later in Checkendon, Oxfordshire,

England. The reception the black troops received from the locals stunned them. The townspeople—many of whom had never seen an African American in person before—greeted them with open arms and treated them like heroes. The residents, who often affectionately referred to the black troops as "tan Yanks," invited them into their homes for cake and tea and even dinner. In nearby villages, pubs, and churches, the soldiers forged new friendships with these nice white folks.

As one correspondent for the *Afro-American*, a newspaper chain for black readers, wrote: "The English people show our lads every possible courtesy and some of the [soldiers], accustomed to ill will, harsh words, and artificial barriers, seem slightly bewildered . . . They never realized there was a part of the world which was willing to forget a man's color and welcome him as a brother."

Here, there were no segregated passenger railcars, no mandatory back-of-the-bus seats, no "colored only" bathrooms, and no forbidden restaurant tables. Many black troops—especially those who grew up in the South—were exposed to freedoms they never had experienced in their own country.

But this warm, liberating feeling didn't last long. As more white American troops arrived in the United Kingdom, they brought their bigotry with them. They slandered African Americans and spread outrageous falsehoods in a devious conspiracy to "re-educate" the Brits, creating a toxic stew that infected many towns and villages. The discriminatory "separate but equal" practices of the US War Department aligned with the thinking of many higher-ups in the British War Cabinet, which concluded it was "desirable that the people of this country should avoid becoming too friendly with colored American troops."

Still, many locals embraced the "tan Yanks" of the 320th. Women organized dances for the troops, who always contributed to the cause by bringing army-issued canned fruit and vegetables, considered luxuries to Brits living on food rations.

Woodson became good friends with the Checkendon postmistress and her husband, who was a fighter pilot for the Royal Air Force. Once, while Woodson was dancing with her, she asked, "Why are your white officers saying such terrible things about Negroes?"

"Prejudice," he replied. "It's ingrained in my country."

But everyone had to move past the racial tensions of the day because they all shared a common goal: Win the war. For the invasion, the men of the 320th learned to deploy VLAs (very low altitude balloons the size of Volkswagens), which were smaller, lighter, more versatile, and required less hydrogen than the regular barrage balloons. The VLAs could be inflated in England and, when attached to landing craft, could be easily transported across the English Channel and set up on the shores of Normandy with only two or three men each rather than four or five.

During the days leading up to D-Day, Woodson wondered if the invasion would be a romp as some optimists predicted or a bloodbath as many feared. *I think it's going to be bad, really bad,* he told himself. He also wondered if he would need to use the German he had learned in high school. *I hope not, because if I have to speak German, it probably means I've been captured.*

Aware of the possibility that he might not come back alive, Woodson wrote a letter to his namesake father, a longtime postal employee, thanking him for all "the little things and the big things you have done for me" as a parent. He wrote in part: "My first year at college you practically paid all the expenses, hoping that I would be able to receive a better education than you have. You always wanted to see that Lloyd [Woodson's brother who was in the army air forces] and I had more advantages than most fellows, so that we could start where you left off. Sometimes it was a sacrifice to do some things for me.

"I know, Dad, that while we're here, you and all the families are behind us. I know it wasn't easy to give up two sons to the US military, but we are here to finish a job which was not done before, so that we can make the world safe for future generations."

It wasn't lost on Woodson that he and his fellow African Americans would be fighting for many of the same liberties that their own country was denying them. But he had no second thoughts about this war. He was willing to do anything—including sacrificing his own life—to help stop the Nazis' quest for global racial supremacy.

As the invasion forces left England on the night of June 5, the 621 men of the 320th and their VLAs were scattered among 150 landing crafts bound for Omaha Beach and Utah

Beach, where they would provide a lethal aerial curtain against the Luftwaffe, the German air force. Before departing, Woodson's pal Cleveland Hayes told him, "If a Nazi bird nestles in my lines, he won't nestle anywhere else."

Woodson and four battalion medics were transported in an LCT that carried a Sherman tank, two jeeps, three trucks (including one with medical supplies), 25 sailors, 30 soldiers, and a crew of 12. During the night crossing of the English Channel, Woodson thought about home—and how he wished he could be there. He didn't talk much; few on board did. The only real sounds came from overhead—the constant drone of Allied planes carrying bombs, paratroopers, and supplies. When dawn broke, the noise erupted into deafening booms from the big guns of battleships, thunderous explosions from dropped bombs, and the reverberating *pow-pow-pow* from German antiaircraft artillery.

I might make it, I might not, but I can't worry about it, he thought. He was glad he had written that letter to his father. If Woodson had to die, at least he had left nothing unsaid to his parents.

Then came the onslaught targeting his ship. In the minutes after the Germans pummeled his LCT with direct hits, more than half the men on board had been killed. The thought that he, too, might soon be among the dead dominated Woodson's mind as he tried to stem the bleeding from the shrapnel that had torn into his lower extremities.

Medic Warren Capers, who had hid inside the medical

supply truck during the attack, jumped out and examined Woodson. "You've got some mean wounds," Capers said. "It ain't fatal, but it ain't good. I'll fix you up as best I can."

After Capers bandaged the gashes, the pain grew worse. *I can't sit around here and mope about it*, Woodson thought. *I've got to start treating the others. Maybe it'll take my mind off the pain.* Limping in agony, he joined Capers and medics Eugene Worthy and Alfred Bell in giving aid to the wounded. Among the few who weren't hurt were three men inside the Sherman tank that the vessel was carrying.

No longer shelled, the smoking LCT finally beached itself more than a mile away from its intended landing spot. The ship's ramp dropped and the tank rolled out. After the medics grabbed supplies, they jumped into four feet of water and plodded toward shore, staying right behind the tank and using it for cover. Every step was excruciating for Woodson, but he pushed forward. On the way in, he plucked a rolled-up tent out of the surf.

Once the tank arrived on the beach, it turned right. The exposed medics made a beeline through enemy fire for the protective base of a cliff. Hobbling, Woodson brought up the rear. They all made it safely just in time to see the tank burst into flames from an artillery shell that blew off the turret. None of the men inside survived.

The injured Woodson helped his comrades set up a first aid station and tent under an outcropping that shielded them from the line of fire. In the chaos, several traumatized soldiers (none from the 320th), including some who had lost their weapons, had become separated from their units and were huddled among the casualties. When an officer from another battalion ordered them to assault a nearby bluff, the men refused because they were too scared and shouted, "We don't want to die!" Others prayed aloud.

Woodson understood their fear. He was scared, too. But he wouldn't let that emotion nor his injuries slow him down. Time and again, he and his fellow medics from the 320th defied the bullets and crawled out into the killing zone to drag the wounded and the dead back to the tent. The medics wore armbands with a red cross indicating they should not be considered targets, according to the Geneva Convention, but German snipers shot at them anyway. Luckily, the enemy kept missing.

Hour after hour, Woodson fought through his pain while treating the fallen. He yanked bullets out of stomachs, arms, and legs. He bandaged gashes and burns from shrapnel. He comforted the dying and injected them with morphine. He gave blood plasma to those who had a fighting chance at surviving. He helped evacuate casualties. The only time he took a brief break was to change the blood-soaked dressings on his own wounds.

All the men Woodson treated were white, but this time—in the middle of battle—no one cared about the color of his skin. They just wanted him to save their lives. At one point, he retrieved several cases of blood marked "Colored" that had floated ashore. Whenever he was working on a wounded man who needed blood, Woodson pointed to the case of African American blood to see if the soldier would refuse it. No one ever did.

The casualties kept mounting, prompting Woodson to ask, "Is there no end?" He worked tirelessly through the rest of the day, night, and following morning. Going beyond exhaustion, he was toiling on automatic pilot.

Around 3 p.m., after 30 excruciating hours during which he had treated more than 200 men, Woodson could do no more and collapsed. After he was revived, he was ordered to get some needed rest.

The tired medic tottered along the beach, hoping to find blankets to use as bedding when he heard shouts for help. They were coming from British troops who had just reached the shore from a landing craft. The man rope, which ran from the vessel to an anchor on the beach, had snapped. Several soldiers who were using it as a lifeline had gone under the surface and were trapped by the weight of their gear.

Woodson lurched into the surf and, one at a time, pulled out four men who had stopped breathing. He lay them on the sand. Forgetting about his fatigue, he dropped to his knees and began cardiopulmonary resuscitation (CPR) on the first unconscious man until the soldier began coughing and spitting out water. While Woodson treated the next victim, he noticed that other Brits had hauled several more unresponsive troops out of the water. "I can't get to them all in time," he told the rescuers. "You're going to have to do artificial respiration yourselves."

"But we don't know how," replied one of the soldiers.

Woodson barked out instructions to the rescuers while he continued doing chest compressions on the second victim, who was soon revived. Then Woodson moved on to the third and fourth men and saved them, too. His directives to the rescuers were spot on; all those men survived.

The gutsy medic passed out again. This time, he was taken to a hospital ship, where he remained for three days. The doctors wanted to keep him in bed longer, but he insisted on returning to his first aid station. "I'm fine," he told them. "I can't do any good here. Let me go." After they released him against their better judgment, Woodson returned to the beach, where he treated the wounded for 12 straight hours until he was overcome by exhaustion.

Woodson and his unit stayed in Normandy for several months. When he finally found time to write home, he said little about his valor on D-Day. His family didn't learn the details until war correspondents found out about his exploits and wrote about him. He was unaware of the articles until one day in September, when his father sent him a letter accompanied by a clipping from the Pittsburgh *Courier*, an African American newspaper, of a front-page story about Woodson's D-Day feats. The headline was simple and to the point: "Hero No. 1 of Invasion."

*   *   *

The 320th Barrage Balloon Battalion performed magnificently on D-Day, providing a defensive aerial wall above Omaha and Utah Beaches that helped protect troop landings and the unloading of supplies. That day, the 621-man unit lost three men while getting hundreds of balloons ashore and aloft under savage artillery, machine gun, and rifle fire.

General Dwight D. Eisenhower, Supreme Commander of the Allied Expeditionary Force, hailed the 320th in a commendation to the men for the "splendid manner" in which they raised their balloons in the face of constant danger. Wrote Eisenhower to the battalion's commanding officer, "Despite the losses sustained, the battalion carried out its mission with courage and determination, and proved an important element of the air defense team . . . I commend you and the officers and men of your battalion for your fine effort which has merited the praise of all who have observed it."

Woodson and three other medics—Warren Capers, Eugene Worthy, and Alfred Bell—received the Bronze Star, the military's fourth-highest combat medal, for their lifesaving actions on D-Day.

After the war, Woodson completed his college education and became a medical technologist at the National Naval Medical Center in Bethesda, Maryland. Then, from 1959 until his retirement in 1980, he worked as a supervisor in the clinical pathology department at the National Institutes of Health.

He and his wife, Joann, had three children, six grandchildren, and thirteen great-grandchildren. Woodson died in 2005 at the age of 83 and was buried in Arlington National Cemetery.

More than one million African Americans served in World War II. However, not one received the Medal of Honor, the military's highest combat award, until after an independent army investigation in 1993 concluded that widespread racism was to blame. (More than 450 Medals of Honor were awarded to white servicemen for their valor in the war.) Hoping to right a wrong, President Bill Clinton in 1997 awarded the Medal of Honor to seven black World War II veterans. Only one of them was still alive to receive it.

Woodson was not among the honorees, although author and researcher Linda Hervieux uncovered a revealing memo in the Harry S. Truman Presidential Library that indicates the medic was considered for the medal. Written in 1945 to a White House aide, the memo said Woodson's commanding officer had recommended him for the Distinguished Service Cross, the second-highest combat medal, but that the office of General John C. H. Lee had upgraded it to the Medal of Honor. No one knows what, if anything, happened afterward. Unfortunately, Woodson's military records, like millions of others, were lost in a devastating fire at the National Personnel Records Center in St. Louis in 1973. Because the army required more documentation than a single memo, it took no further action on a possible upgrade to Woodson's medal.

In recalling his D-Day experience several years before his death, Woodson wrote, "This was a horrible day for everyone. This D-Day, army prejudices took a backseat, as far as the soldiers helping one another was concerned. However, afterwards it was an altogether different story. Even to this day, the black soldiers were never given credit for their outstanding services beyond the call of duty."

You will find more information about the remarkable brave men of the 320th Barrage Balloon Battalion in the book Forgotten: The Untold Story of D-Day's Black Heroes, at Home and at War by Linda Hervieux (HarperCollins).

KILLER INSTINCT

STAFF SERGEANT HARRISON SUMMERS
1st Battalion, 502nd Parachute Infantry Regiment,
101st Airborne Division

O n the massive nighttime airlift over the English Channel that would drop 13,000 paratroopers into German-occupied France in the dead of night, Staff Sergeant Harrison Summers didn't say much. Few of his comrades did. They were lost in their own thoughts while sitting on hard benches inside their droning two-engine C-47.

Summers closed his eyes and conjured up memories of his childhood in Marion County, West Virginia, where he used to skinny-dip in the Monongahela River and fish along its banks. He replayed in his mind the good times he had at East Fairmont High School and the not-so-good times working in the coal mine in Rivesville after graduation. He was sure he made the right decision when he enlisted in the army in peacetime, in 1937, at the age of 19.

Now here he was, seven years later, a well-trained paratrooper assigned to the 1st Battalion, 502nd Parachute Infantry Regiment of the 101st Airborne Division, poised to do his part in spearheading the Allied invasion.

The soft-spoken, broad-shouldered 26-year-old former coal miner wasn't so much scared as he was curious about how he would react in his first encounter with the Germans. He knew his quiet nature and live-and-let-live attitude would be sorely tested. Could he kill another human being—someone's son, brother, husband, father—simply because the guy was wearing a different uniform? That's what Summers had been trained to do, kill the enemy. But, he wondered, would he hesitate for just a second before pulling the trigger? Would he spare the life of a wounded or unarmed German soldier?

"Five minutes to the drop zone," the jumpmaster alerted the paratroopers.

Summers made a final check of the 70 pounds of gear he was carrying—backpack, gas mask, rifle, first aid kit, food, clothing, ammunition, parachute. And his cricket. He knew the small metal toy, which made a clicking sound when pressed, could be a lifesaver. Each trooper carried at least one, which he clicked in the dark to identify himself as an American to other Americans. One click meant, "Is anyone near me?" Two clicks was a reply, "Yes, a friend." *I sure don't want to lose my cricket*, he thought.

As the planes carrying the sky soldiers began swooping over the Normandy coast, they encountered fog and antiaircraft fire, forcing many of them to break formation, which fouled up timing and location. As a result, thousands of paratroopers were missing their assigned landing zones and ending up lost and scattered over wide areas far from their units.

Hundreds upon hundreds were dropping into enemy strongholds where they were easily captured or killed. Some were landing in flooded meadows where they were unable to free themselves before drowning. Many others were coming down on rooftops of barns or houses or landing high in the trees.

Summers and his comrades didn't know any of that. They were dealing with their own problem. The flight commander had given the order for the paratroopers to jump, but they couldn't because a bundle of supplies that needed to be shoved out first was stuck and blocked the doorway. Several crucial minutes passed before the troopers could free it. By the time they could jump, they all assumed the delay meant they would land way off course.

When it was his turn to leap from the plane, Summers didn't hesitate. He sailed out the open doorway into the darkness and the unknown. Because of all the gear he was carrying, he hit the ground hard but wasn't hurt because he rolled as he was taught. He hurried to unhitch himself from his parachute while warily looking out for the enemy.

To his welcome surprise, he discovered that he was dropped close to his designated area. The flight commander had erred, which turned out to be a lucky break. Had the men jumped when he first told them to, they would have missed their drop zone by miles. But the delay put them near where they needed to be. *We got lucky when the cargo got stuck*, Summers thought.

He met up with three paratroopers who, like him,

were looking for the command post, which, if all went according to plan, would be near the coastal village of Saint-Germain-de-Varreville.

As the four men walked down a lane lined with hedgerows, Summers halted his comrades. "I heard something," he whispered, pointing to a spot about 10 yards ahead on the other side of the hedgerow. Then he heard a click. Summers clicked back twice.

From behind a tree, out stepped an American paratrooper. In the moonlight, Summers recognized him. He was 24-year-old Staff Sergeant Roy Nickrent, the operations sergeant in Summers's battalion. "Oh, am I glad to see you boys," Nickrent said in a quiet voice. "I thought you were Krauts. I was getting ready to shoot. Where are we?"

After they told him, Nickrent said, "My plane was way off course when we jumped. It was flying so low that my parachute barely had time to open. I landed in a tree and got stuck about twenty feet up. I couldn't get out of my harness, and I heard the Krauts nearby, so I used my knife to cut myself free from my chute and dropped to the ground. I was afraid I had given away my position because I made a loud noise when I landed, so then I crawled to a gully and tried to gather my wits. That's when I heard footsteps and thought, 'I'm gonna kill 'em or they're gonna kill me.' I'm sure happy it's you."

He joined the others, who continued quietly down the lane. As they entered a deserted hamlet, they stopped in their tracks. There, ahead of them, were the bodies of two American paratroopers hanging in the trees by their parachutes. "Those lousy Germans shot them dead before they could even hit the ground," Summers muttered. "The Krauts didn't have the decency to take them prisoner."

They moved farther into the hamlet, where they saw the results of more sickening German atrocities against US soldiers, who had been tortured before they were killed. "Butchers," Summers spat. He could feel an unfamiliar rage churning inside him. Any lingering doubt that he would pause for even a millisecond before killing the enemy had vanished.

The five soon reached the command post headed by Lieutenant Colonel Patrick Cassidy, the commanding officer of the 1st Battalion. Cassidy and his unit were given two major D-Day objectives: Secure defensive positions north of Causeway 4—a road that led from Utah Beach to the interior—and capture a German barracks compound that housed nearly 200 heavily armed members of a strategic artillery battery of 122mm guns near the village of Saint-Martin-de-Varreville, about a mile from the beach.

The complex, which was designated on Allied invasion maps as WXYZ, consisted of 11 farmhouses and buildings scattered along a half-mile stretch. The French farmers, who had built the structures of stone blocks and tile roofs by hand, had lived and worked in them for years until the Germans had seized them for their own use. All but three of the buildings sat on the north side of Reuville Road, a dirt lane lined with thick hedgerows.

It was vital that the Americans capture the enemy compound before the bulk of the invasion force from Utah Beach arrived. But Colonel Cassidy was running out of time and men. He had already dispatched troopers to set up roadblocks north and south of his position and had sent others to form a defensive perimeter to protect the command post. With so many men out on those missions, less than 20 paratroopers remained. And most of them were from various units who didn't know each other. They had found their way here after landing far from their assigned drop zones because their planes had been off course.

Cassidy went over to Summers and ordered, "Your job is to lead a patrol and clear out WXYZ."

Summers, a man of few words, replied, "Yes, sir."

Cassidy selected the only men he could spare. Fourteen troopers—all but two were strangers to Summers—were ordered to follow the sergeant. Even though Summers had been in the army for seven years, he felt awkward leading men he had never met before. He didn't know anything about them, especially their fighting abilities. Of course, the same was true for them; they knew nothing about him, so they were leery of his leadership.

Summers didn't fret over the fact that his small force faced daunting odds attacking a full-strength German company that was more than 10 times the size of his. He had his orders, and he intended to carry them out to the best of his ability. Besides, his disgust and hostility toward the Germans was nearing the boiling point.

With images of the disfigured bodies of his fellow paratroopers fresh in his mind, Summers led the new men without taking even a minute to learn their names. As point man, he moved the group swiftly but cautiously along the north hedgerow of Reuville Road until they neared the compound at around 9 a.m. Starting to creep toward the first farmhouse, Summers turned to give directions to the men. But they were reluctant to follow this unfamiliar leader and remained behind the hedgerow in a roadside ditch. *They seem to have little stomach for the fight I'm about to start*, he thought. *I should lead by example. Then maybe they'll follow me.*

Pointing to a slight hill about 50 yards away, he told Sergeant Leland Baker, "Go to the top of the rise and keep a lookout in that direction, and don't let anyone come over that hill and get on my flank. Stay there until you're told to come back." Baker nodded and hustled off.

The farmhouse's thick stone walls were bored with gunports so the Germans could shoot through them toward any exposed Allied troops while being protected from return fire. Seeing the Americans, the enemy began firing away. Bullets ripped into the trees, showering Summers and his men with leaves. *I can't just stay here*, he thought. *I've got to get those Krauts even if I have to do it myself.* He told his men, "Keep firing. Keep them engaged."

While they provided cover fire, Summers low-crawled along a bushy hedge without the Germans spotting him. It was time for this lanky West Virginian to take the fight to the Germans.

Slowly and methodically, he stood up and approached the back door of the farmhouse. He wasn't sure how many Germans were on the other side, but he was sure that he was going to kill them all or die trying. He wrapped his index finger firmly around the trigger of his tommy gun. He inhaled deeply and charged.

Using his shoulder as a battering ram, Summers busted through the wooden door, surprising the 10 Germans who were firing through the gunports. Without saying a word, Summers blasted away at them with his weapon, killing the four closest to him while the others scrambled out through another door.

Sprinting toward the road, some of the Germans turned around to fire at Summers. He ducked out of the way. Then they disappeared through the hedgerow. As he ran after them, he passed by his men, who were firing from the ditch. He said nothing to them, although he thought, *Now will you guys follow me?* Not waiting to see if they would, Summers squirmed through the thick hedgerow and—still alone—sneaked up on the backside of the second farmhouse. He wondered if the Germans were hiding inside. Once again, he rammed open the door, but this time, the enemy wasn't there. *Well, they're not going to escape from me that easily.*

Just then he heard voices from upstairs—a man shouting in French and another one speaking English. Coming down the steps were a middle-aged man dressed in typical farmer's attire and Lieutenant Elmer Brandenberger, an officer from Summers's own Company B. A half hour earlier, Brandenberger and two of his men had tried but failed to drive the Germans out of a different building in the compound before entering this house. The lieutenant looked shaken.

"I was about to let go with a burst of fire upstairs because I saw movement," he told Summers. "For some reason, I hesitated. I took a second look and saw a boy about twelve with a pale face peering at me from under a blanket. Then this Frenchman—I think it's his father—came from another room, pointed at the boy, and shouted at me, '*Malade! Malade!*' Thank goodness I knew that *malade* means 'sick' in French. Harrison, I almost shot a child."

Not in a compassionate mood, Summers dismissed the officer's distress. This was no time for chitchat. "Where are the Germans who ran by here?" he asked bluntly.

"The Frenchman told me the Germans went into the next house."

"I'm going after them," said Summers.

"Alone? Where are your men?"

Summers shrugged.

Hearing machine gun fire at the far end of the compound, Brandenberger said, "I need to find my men and deal with that gun. Reinforcements should be coming soon. If they get here before we can take out that machine gun, they'll get chewed up."

Brandenberger ran off, dodging bullets from the Germans, who were firing out of six gunports from the third farmhouse. *That's my next objective,* Summers thought.

Private William Burt, who was carrying a light machine gun, left the troopers in the roadside ditch and hustled over to Summers. "I thought you could use my help," Burt said.

Summers nodded and said, "I'm going in alone. Lay down suppressing fire."

As Summers began his advance, the Germans tried to stop him with their firepower. But Burt was shooting continuously at the front of the farmhouse, forcing them to keep their heads down and fire blindly at Summers, who zigzagged his way toward the back.

Summers knew he was outnumbered six to one. But he didn't care. Still powered by his loathing for the Germans over their inhumane treatment of his comrades, he kicked open the door and sprayed the inside with his tommy gun, killing all six before they could fire a single shot at him.

Summers then slumped to the floor. He felt neither joy nor sadness in killing those men or the ones in the first house. There was no sense of triumph or gloating. Maybe those feelings would come later after his ongoing rampage was over. But for now, he was on a one-man mission of revenge against the Germans. They were going to pay with their lives for fighting on behalf of a madman, for invading peace-loving countries, for torturing his fellow paratroopers.

Summers started toward the fourth farmhouse when the men from his makeshift squad finally left the ditch and came over to him. After they replenished his supply of ammunition, which was running low, they followed his orders and moved farther down the ditch until they faced the fourth farmhouse.

Then, on his signal, they provided cover fire as he dashed toward the back. *Do or die*, he thought. He flung himself against the door, not realizing it was unlatched. He lurched into the house, lost his balance, and stumbled to the floor. For a second, he thought he'd be killed, but after scrambling to his feet, he discovered the house was empty. Summers then had to duck because several perfectly placed bullets from his men's weapons zinged through the gunports and ricocheted off the interior walls. *I'm safer outside than I am inside*, he thought.

Leaving the house, Summers encountered a tall, young captain from the 82nd Airborne Division, who had approached him from a nearby orchard. "I was dropped far from my landing zone," the officer said. "I guess fate brought me here to help you." He motioned toward a larger building across the road about 100 yards away. It served as the German officers' quarters. "I saw some Krauts running from this house toward that building," the captain said.

"I don't know how many are inside, but we need to take

them out," replied Summers. After signaling his men in the ditch to direct their cover fire at the quarters, Summers sprang from a hedgerow and began streaking across an open area. The captain kept pace with him. Despite the Americans' suppressing fire, the Germans let loose with a volley of bullets. Summers was halfway to the building when he heard a loud groan. Turning around, he saw the captain sprawled on his back on the ground. *He's shot!* Summers hurried back to him, hoping to drag him away from the killing zone. When he reached him, Summers dropped to his knees and saw that the captain had been fatally shot through the heart. *I never even got his name.*

The sight of another dead American further fueled Summers's quest to kill the Germans. Pleased that Private Burt and the others were laying down the heaviest cover fire yet, Summers got up and charged the officers' quarters alone. He didn't need to muster up courage or vengeance. He had plenty of both. Like before, he barged through the back door and let loose with his tommy gun. Dodging return fire, he shot one German, then another and another until six fell. Ten others poured out a side door and then raised their hands in surrender.

Aiming his weapon at them, Summers almost wished they hadn't laid down their arms. Fury was still roiling in his veins, and he wanted to kill them all. But he knew he couldn't now that they had given up. His restraint reminded him that he still possessed some humanity.

Seeing what he had done, Summers's men rushed out of the ditch, and then some of them took the prisoners away. Amazed at his actions, Private John Camien, one of the members of the hodgepodge group, asked him, "Why are you doing all of this?"

"I can't tell you," mumbled Summers, who was squatting in a baseball catcher's stance, his eyes staring at nothing. It takes a lot out of a man when he repeatedly bursts through the door of the enemy, not knowing what's on the other side, or how much firepower he's about to face, or whether he's seconds away from death.

"What do you want the rest of us to do?" Camien asked.

Summers shrugged and replied, "Most of you don't seem to want to fight. And I can't make you. I intend to finish what I started. Alone."

Holding up his carbine, Camien said, "Well, not anymore. I'm sticking with you."

Summers nodded in appreciation. Turning to Private Burt, who had been delivering needed cover fire from his light machine gun from different positions, Summers said, "We're going to clean out the rest of the buildings one at a time. Move on down the ditch with the other men and keep up a steady stream of suppressing fire as we go into each one."

Summers and Camien then broke into the next three farmhouses. In each case, the Germans were so focused on firing back at the Americans in the ditch that the enemy didn't notice the two attackers until it was too late. By the time the pair had cleared those houses, they had killed 15 more Germans. *Three buildings left*, Summers thought.

He and Camien then moved farther west toward the ninth structure in the compound, a building that had been turned into the mess hall for the enlisted men of the German artillery group. Nearby, Summers's makeshift group, including Private Burt, followed along the ditch, where they were joined by several reinforcements sent by Colonel Cassidy to help capture WXYZ. But they remained in the ditch, which was nearly 100 yards away from the mess hall. None of them wanted to storm it, especially after seeing what had happened to Lieutenant Brandenberger minutes earlier.

He had tried to take out a machine gun nest in the courtyard in front of the building. But even though he was backed by suppressing fire, he was struck by a flurry of bullets that mangled his arm. The officer staggered back to the ditch before he passed out.

Summers and Camien chose to attack the mess hall, but from a different direction than Brandenberger had tried. As they neared a side door, Summers whispered to Camien, "I'm going in. Cover me."

Summers kicked open the door and immediately began firing his tommy gun at everyone inside. At first, his brain couldn't grasp at what he was seeing. It made no sense. Unbelievably, more than a dozen German artillerymen were seated at mess tables, eating their lunch rather than defending their compound. It was as if they were oblivious to all the shooting that had been going on outside. As the startled Germans tried to reach for their weapons, Summers continued to blast away until every one of them was slumped across a table, slouched over a chair, or lying on the floor, lifeless.

He took no satisfaction slaying the enemy this way other than to think, *There's another dozen or so Krauts who won't be shooting Americans.* He was feeling shaky, having once again escaped death. No one would have questioned him if he quit now and let someone else take over. But there were still two more buildings left—a long two-story enlisted men's stone barracks and a large wooden shed off to the side. Unlike the occupants in the mess hall, the Germans inside the building were firing out of windows and gunports at the Americans who were shooting at them from the ditch. The Germans had the advantage because the barracks was situated on a gentle hill that overlooked an open area more than 50 yards from the hedgerow where Summers and Camien were plotting their attack. Surveying the area, Summers said, "There's no cover for us from any direction. If we try to run across the open area, we'll get mowed down for sure."

Meanwhile, more reinforcements began to arrive. But as they stepped out from the orchard, a sniper in a tree shot at them from behind, killing three. When the others dived into the hedgerow on the opposite side, they found themselves exposed to the German gunmen in the barracks. Bullets tore into eight Americans, fatally wounding four of them. The others were carried down the road to safety while Summers's group provided covering fire.

Summers noticed a haystack next to the shed, which was only a few feet away from the barracks. He motioned for Private Burt to maneuver to a better vantage point and pointed to the haystack. Burt understood the message. Using tracer ammo, Burt fired into the haystack, setting it ablaze. The flames soon spread to the shed, which, unknown to the Americans, contained ammunition for the German battery.

Within minutes, the inferno reached the artillery shells that were stored inside. One by one, they exploded, launching orange balls of fire high into the air. About 50 Germans had been hiding in the shed, waiting to slaughter the Americans during an all-out assault. But when the shed went up in flames, the Germans bailed out, firing their weapons willy-nilly as they tried to run across the open ground. Although the soldiers in the barracks next door had opened up a vicious fusillade that kept the Americans pinned down, the paratroopers still killed about 30 escaping Germans.

Soon, Staff Sergeant Roy Nickrent, lugging a bazooka, arrived and worked his way along a hedgerow near the mess hall, where Summers and Camien were holed up. Summers nodded at Nickrent but didn't say anything. There was no need. Nickrent knew what to do. From his position, he fired several rounds at the barracks, but they landed short. Meanwhile, the Germans' firepower foiled any possible attack by the Americans. Neither side wanted to venture into No Man's Land.

With each round from his bazooka, Nickrent adjusted his aim until the seventh one crashed right through the roof. Seconds later, thick black smoke began pouring out of the hole.

As the flames spread inside, the Germans stopped shooting from their gunports and began running out of the burning building. While attempting to escape across the open field, they shot blindly toward the Americans' position only to get caught in a crossfire with Summers and his men, who were shooting from a hedge off the right flank.

The fleeing Germans wouldn't stop shooting, so neither would the Americans. It was almost too easy for the paratroopers. Finally, after about 50 Germans lay on the ground dead, the rest of the soldiers in the barracks—31 of them—emerged with their hands raised in surrender.

The capture of WXYZ was over. The large German unit that had posed a menacing threat to the Allied invasion forces landing at Utah Beach had been seized.

For Summers, it had been nearly five grueling hours since he was ordered to lead the nerve-racking mission of clearing out the compound with an undermanned, underperforming force. Time and again, he had attacked the enemy virtually by himself. Now that he had single-handedly killed about 30 Germans and helped capture more than 40 others, he couldn't savor this victory. He was too exhausted physically, too worn down mentally, too wiped out emotionally.

Summers sat on the ground, his head buried between his

raised knees, and began to tremble. Nickrent came over, patted him on the back, and asked, "How do you feel?"

Looking up with bloodshot eyes, Summers replied, "Not very good. It was all so crazy. I'm sure I'll never do anything like this again."

For his courageous actions on D-Day, Summers earned the Distinguished Service Cross. He also was given a battlefield commission to lieutenant. During the following months, he received Purple Hearts after he was wounded twice, once during Operation Market Garden in Holland and again during the Siege of Bastogne in Belgium.

After the war, Summers returned to Marion County, West Virginia, where he raised a family and worked as a coal miner and later as a coal mine inspector. "When it came to the war, he didn't want to talk about it," his son Richard told the Charleston Gazette-Mail in 1999. "That was in the past."

In the same article, Jim Sago, a friend of Summers, recalled, "Many of the men who worked with Harrison in the Marion coal mines didn't even know he had fought in World War II. He was once even left out of a veterans' appreciation day at the mine. He never marched in parades or wore his medals or anything."

Summers died from lung cancer in 1983 and was buried at Beverly Hills Memorial Park in nearby Morgantown.

"THE UNSINKABLE IS SINKING!"

ENSIGN JOSEPH "JOE" ALEXANDER
Navy LCT 856

Think, think!" Joe Alexander muttered to himself. "I've got to find a way to save us."

His mission was not going according to the plan. In fact, nothing was going right and everything was going wrong.

As skipper of a landing craft, he was in charge of delivering the soldiers and equipment on board to an area of Omaha Beach that was supposed to have been secured. But it wasn't. And now his ship was trapped in a whirlpool of death and destruction.

Enemy artillery rounds were pounding his ship, killing and wounding his seamen and soldiers, igniting fires, disabling his guns, ripping holes in his hull, and flooding his engine room. Without power or an anchor, the sinking vessel was drifting closer to shore, coming perilously within range of German machine guns, grenades, and the shelling from a tank that likely could finish off not only the boat but also everyone on board.

Although his craft was powerless, he wasn't—at least that's what he told himself. There had to be a way to save his men. "Think, think!"

War was the farthest thing from Alexander's mind when, fresh out of high school, he enrolled at Butler University in his hometown of Indianapolis in 1941. He had visions of becoming a businessman one day. But then Japan attacked Pearl Harbor, triggering the United States' entry into World War II. Wanting to do his part to defend America, the teenager quit college and enlisted in the navy, which thought he had the potential to be an officer. It sent him to the University of Notre Dame Midshipman School, where he and hundreds of other candidates had to cram the lessons of a four-year training program into three months. After completing the condensed course, he was commissioned an ensign. To veteran sailors, he and others like him were nothing more than wet-behind-the-ears "90-Day Wonders."

Despite the brief navy schooling, Alexander impressed his superiors. After further training, he became skipper of a special type of ship known as an LCT, short for "landing craft for tanks." One of nearly 500 built in the US for the navy, this flat-bottom amphibious assault vessel was designed to deliver tanks, military vehicles, and troops onto a beachhead without the need for a harbor. Her job was to deliberately run aground where she would open her bow, drop a ramp, and unload her cargo, which could be as many as four tanks or a combination of troops, equipment, and vehicles. Her powerful three engines would then go in reverse and pull the 112-foot-long craft off the beach and out into the open water.

Alexander never felt prouder than he did on the day he took command of LCT 856. So what if she was ugly and slow and was mockingly called "Long Crawling Target." So what if the pokey work vessel was cramped and uncomfortable for the young skipper and his 16-member crew. He didn't mind because this was his ship. To him, she was beautiful.

Before seeing any action in the war, Alexander and his men needed more training in England to prepare for the invasion at Normandy. Because the LCT had a range of only 700 miles, she and her crew were transported across the Atlantic aboard a much larger cargo ship. During the 19-day transatlantic journey, some sailors questioned whether Alexander was physically able to be a skipper. The seas were so rough that he suffered a severe bout of seasickness every day of the entire voyage. How, they wondered, could this green-around-the-gills ensign command a ship if he couldn't stomach storm-tossed waters?

He soon allayed concerns after LCT 856 was craned off the cargo ship and put in the harbor at Plymouth, England. From the moment he took control of his vessel, Alexander never experienced any *mal de mer* again because he focused solely on his job. A gung-ho, by-the-book skipper, he impressed his superiors with his seamanship and leadership during training exercises off the English coast, which were more dangerous than anticipated.

In April 1944, the Allies conducted Exercise Tiger, a series of secret rehearsals for the impending D-Day invasion. To get raw troops and sailors accustomed to the sound and fury of combat, this training was conducted under live fire conditions. During a mock landing at England's Slapton Beach, friendly fire killed dozens of men.

The next night, on April 28, nine lumbering LSTs—ships similar to LCTs only much bigger—were carrying thousands of troops when they were attacked in Lyme Bay by a German flotilla of swift torpedo vessels known as E-boats. The hit-and-run ambush destroyed two LSTs, severely damaged a third, and claimed the lives of 749 American sailors and soldiers.

Despite the devastating attack, the exercises continued. Two days later, Alexander's vessel joined a convoy of LCTs that followed a British destroyer in a training mission. The LCTs were ordered to maintain radio silence and follow in single file into Lyme Bay, where enemy boats lurked—a dangerous area in the English Channel known as E-Boat Alley. Shortly after getting underway, they encountered heavy fog. It was so thick that Alexander stationed a seaman on the bow to maintain eye contact with the boat ahead of him. But he soon lost sight of her.

LCT 856 was now on her own in waters where E-boats prowled for easy prey. Because he hadn't been told the destination of the convoy, Alexander decided to find a safe harbor. He coolly guided his ship through the fog, avoiding the Germans as well as British mines, and entered a naval base at the south end of the Portland Peninsula at 1 a.m. the next day.

Later that morning, he reported to headquarters. When

the commander heard what had happened to LCT 856, he told Alexander, "You mean to tell me that you crossed E-Boat Alley unescorted and made it safely here? You must be crazy, lucky, or brave." Alexander liked to think he was brave—and maybe a little lucky.

On June 3, the 21-year-old ensign attended a top secret meeting where he learned details of the D-Day invasion. He saw photos and a clay model of where he would bring LCT 856 to shore—Normandy's Omaha Beach. "Prior to the assault, the beach will be bombed from the air," an officer briefed him. "Our bombers will make five thousand sorties and devastate the enemy positions. The army engineers will then blow open a path fifty yards wide to clear out the underwater obstacles. Your mission is to enter Fox Red at H plus two-twenty. [That meant on the eastern edge of Omaha Beach 2 hours and 20 minutes after the start of the invasion.] Memorize your point of entry to the beach, but only by the contour of the land. All manmade objects—houses, barns, buildings—will have been destroyed. One more thing, Ensign Alexander. You will lead a column of ten LCTs."

The announcement surprised Alexander. *Why does the commander want me in the lead? I'm only an ensign who has never faced combat.* He went to his superior and asked, "Are you sure the navy thinks I'm qualified to be the lead ship? Shouldn't the honor go to someone with more experience?"

"The order came from the commander himself," the officer replied. "He's put you up front because he thinks you are the best person for the job after learning how you skippered your ship through fog and E-Boat Alley. That impressed him. So, Ensign, you're definitely qualified to take the lead position."

Because the skipper was short one officer, headquarters assigned him a young executive officer, Charlie Morgan*, who had just received his commission, exchanged wedding vows, and been shipped to England all within the previous few days.

On June 5, Alexander's LCT was loaded with jeeps, command cars, a few dozen soldiers, and a 32-ton Sherman tank to support members of the 1st Infantry Division, who would begin storming the beach at dawn the next day. Based on the briefing of the upcoming assault, he assumed his craft would be part of an uneventful in-and-out mission. Because the vessel could go only five knots an hour with such a heavy load, she left 26 hours before her scheduled beach landing 110 miles away.

During the crossing of the English Channel, Alexander was in awe of the size of the armada. Ships of all sizes and shapes fore and aft of his little LCT plowed through the waves from horizon to horizon. "What a magnificent sight," he marveled to Morgan. "The Germans are in for a big surprise."

The seas were rough, much like they were during Alexander's stomach-churning transatlantic voyage months earlier. But because he was so keyed up over his first command in combat, he wasn't seasick. That wasn't the case for some members of the crew and many of the soldiers who were upchucking in their helmets throughout the journey.

Morgan, who wasn't bothered by the ship's pitching and

rolling, tried to encourage the ailing men and even joked with them to get their minds off the angry seas. To show what kind of officer he was, he washed dishes, secured the galley, and did other tasks that crewmen were too sick to do.

By daylight, LCT 856 had reached the Normandy coast and began circling, waiting for her assigned time to plow into the beach and deliver her cargo and soldiers. Brimming with confidence, Alexander thought, *Hey, you Krauts. We are the Americans. You better lay down your guns and run.*

But soon he was startled to see so much enemy resistance. Artillery shells were exploding in the water port and starboard. Machine guns from pillboxes and bunkers on shore were spraying their deadly bullets as soldiers by the thousands poured out of Allied landing craft that had rammed into sandbars and beaches. US destroyers and battleships cruising offshore kept up a steady barrage from their big guns. Based on what he had heard at the briefing a few days earlier, Alexander assumed the beach would be secure. Clearly, it wasn't. *I sure didn't expect this*, he thought.

Although he was alarmed by all the chaos and fighting and explosions, the young ensign wasn't deterred. About 2,000 yards off the shore, his boat reached the rendezvous area on time. He expected the other LCTs to fall in line behind him, ready to hit the beach. But they weren't moving in a way that indicated they were prepared for the run-up. Perplexed, Alexander shouted through a megaphone to the skipper behind him, "Why aren't the other boats lining up?"

"They're all scared to go in," came the reply. "It's not safe yet for them or the soldiers."

What a bunch of baloney, Alexander thought. The answer disgusted him so much that he didn't even respond. *Let's hope when they see what my crew and I do, they'll follow. We have our orders, and we intend to carry them out.* He turned to his helmsman and ordered, "Steer her toward the beach. Full speed ahead!"

LCT 856 turned and slammed into the waves, crossing the bow of the battleship *Arkansas,* whose big guns were booming nonstop. After each 14-inch shell was fired, smoke poured out of the barrels and engulfed Alexander's boat in a choking shroud so dense he couldn't see his hand in front of his face until the LCT had moved past the battleship.

Stationed on the conning tower, a raised platform at the stern of his craft, Alexander now had a good view of the assault. The death and destruction unfolding on Omaha Beach didn't faze him at first because he was operating with confidence. *Nothing will stop me,* he told himself. *I'll go in, unload, back off, and continue on to my next assignment. So far, all is perfect, the timing and our position.*

As the LCT drew closer to shore, he was surprised to see that a house on a ridge above the beach directly in line with his craft was still standing. *That should have been destroyed,* he thought. A lieutenant colonel, who was in charge of the soldiers aboard the vessel, rushed up the ladder to the conning tower and told Alexander, "You can't go in there! Look at our boys on the beach!"

Convinced the officer was chickening out, Alexander barked, "Get off of my conning tower! I'll have none of this cowardice aboard my ship!"

"My men will get slaughtered!" the colonel shouted.

Alexander hadn't paid close attention to the soldiers on the beach because he was concentrating so much on getting his LCT to shore. What he saw stunned him. Hundreds of soldiers were facedown, hugging the beach behind the shingle, which was getting raked by machine gun fire. He could see the soles of their shoes. *It's like they're holding on with their fingernails,* he thought. *The colonel is right. I can't let them off yet. The beach isn't secure.*

The LCT continued toward the shore. *I need to at least unload the tank and then back off the beach and wait until it's safer for these boys to get off.*

The approach toward Fox Red was spot on. When the craft was less than 100 yards from the beach, a gunner on one of the LCT's two 20mm guns asked the skipper for permission to open fire.

"To fire at what?" Alexander asked.

"The house up ahead," the gunner replied. "The Germans are firing at us from there."

"Open fire!" the skipper ordered.

With his megaphone, Alexander called out to a crewmember who was standing by the bow, gawking at the firefight on the beach, "Lay low!"

But the seaman, who was manning the anchor winch,

thought the ensign said, "Let go." He released the anchor, which snagged onto a sandbar, bringing the craft to a halt farther out than Alexander had planned. *Since the anchor is down, there's nothing I can do about it now,* he told himself. *At least we're close enough to get the tank off.*

But before he could utter the command to lower the ramp, an 88mm artillery shell struck the port gun, seriously wounding the gunner and his two loaders. The force of the blast knocked several seamen to the deck. Alexander scrambled off the conning tower to check on the condition of the wounded. Several were bleeding and burned. A medic attached to the group of soldiers sprinted over to provide emergency aid.

As the skipper rushed back toward the conning tower, another 88mm enemy round landed on board, this time near the wheelhouse. The blast knocked Alexander down and dazed him. When he got to his feet, he saw five seamen stagger out. All were bleeding badly. Then another shell exploded on the LCT on the port side.

Alexander dashed inside the smoking, damaged wheelhouse and took over the controls, which, despite the shelling, were still working. He thrust the engines in reverse, gripped the wheel, and tried to operate the radio all at the same time. The radio was too damaged to send out a distress call. After turning the craft around, he tried to head out to sea but couldn't make any headway. *The anchor is holding us back! I've got to cut the cable.*

As he dashed out of the wheelhouse toward the cable cutter, a fourth shell struck on the starboard side, injuring more sailors and seamen. By now, two fires, one amidships and the other toward the bow, had flared up and were growing. *No time for fighting fires*, he thought. *Let somebody else put them out. I've got to keep us from drifting back to the beach. If we get any closer, we'll be in range of machine guns.*

He grasped the metal cutter, which required him to place it over the one-inch cable and then pound it with a sledgehammer until the cable was severed. He started striking the cable cutter with all his strength. Over and over, he swung the heavy sledgehammer but couldn't break the line. Out of the corner of his eye, he saw enemy tracer bullets whizz by him. *We're in range.*

Suddenly, a seaman ran over to him and announced, "The engine rooms are flooded!" Alexander handed the sledgehammer to another crewman and yelled, "Cut us free!" Then the ensign hurried below, noticing blood of the wounded smeared on bulkheads and the deck.

At the hatch to the auxiliary room, Alexander encountered a machinist who was standing on a ladder that led down to the generator room. "Get down there and see what the situation is," the skipper ordered.

The seaman shook his head and said, "People are drowning down there."

No time to argue. In frustration, Alexander grabbed the sailor by the hair and yanked him off the ladder. Then the skipper scurried down the ladder and waded in waist-high water to the flooded generator room. He saw that a shell had made a hole in the bulkhead, allowing water to gush in from the engine room, where the engines were underwater and inoperable.

Although the builders of the vessel claimed she was unsinkable because the hull was constructed with 32 separate watertight compartments, the craft began listing. "The unsinkable is sinking!" Alexander growled to no one in particular.

The anchor, which had kept the LCT from backing off the sandbar, was now the only thing preventing the craft from drifting straight onto the beach, where she would be an even easier target than she already was. *I've got to stop the cable from being cut!*

He hustled back topside and noticed a dead soldier slumped over in his jeep. *His poor family. The heartache they'll suffer when they find out he's dead.*

When Alexander reached the cable cutter, he groaned. He was too late. The cable had been severed. LCT 856 was now powerless and lifeless. *There's no way to stop us from floating back to the beach. Wait. Maybe there is another way . . .*

He dashed over to the port side, where a spare anchor was stored. He discovered that an artillery shell had embedded itself in the anchor, almost breaking it in half. *It's better than nothing. If I tie a rope to it and push it off the side, will it hold?* He didn't get his answer because the anchor was too heavy for him and a seaman to lift. "It's no use," the skipper said. "I'll have to think of something else."

The wind and current had turned the craft, leaving her

starboard side fully exposed to enemy fire. The port side was already pitted with hundreds of holes from machine gun bullets. For the first time, Alexander felt he might lose his ship, his crewmen, the soldiers—and his life.

I've got to stop the boat from floating back into the beach. In desperation, he grabbed a throw line, a sturdy long rope that had a knot on one end called a monkey fist. Paying little attention to the bullets, he stood on the bow, waiting for a landing craft to come near. He was hoping to toss the throw line to another skipper, who would take it and tow out LCT 856.

But because of the mass confusion and intense firepower of the German artillery and machine guns, not a single craft was heading toward Fox Red. The boats either had already dropped off their soldiers or were waiting until it was safer to come ashore. No one was willing or able to help.

The sinking LCT continued to drift with the current until the bottom of the hull finally settled in three-foot-deep water to the east of her original destination. That turned into a lucky break because she was beached in the shadow of a cliff, which Alexander figured would protect him and his men from some enemy fire.

But the Germans on top of the cliff began hurling grenades at them and moving a tank into position to shoot at the stricken craft. Fortunately, an American destroyer just offshore started firing her guns, dueling with the tank and forcing the rest of the Germans there to retreat.

When the destroyer's five-inch shells exploded, they shook

the ground and made earth and rocks tumble down the cliff face and onto the beach. While the destroyer was occupying the enemy, Alexander ordered the LCT's bow opened and ramp deployed. Then the soldiers who weren't wounded ran ashore while the lone American tank and other vehicles were offloaded.

At least I got the men and equipment off the boat, Alexander thought. *But I have to help all the wounded.* He ran west along the beach. Even though more fighting was going on there, he figured he had a better chance of finding medical aid or a vessel that could take his wounded.

He looked out to sea and spotted a lone Higgins boat—a much smaller landing craft than his LCT—coming toward him to offload her 36 soldiers. *This is great. Once they're all off, I'll get the skipper to pick up my wounded.*

When the Higgins boat was about 100 yards from him, he began waving his arms to get the skipper's attention. Suddenly, an enormous explosion at the bow of the boat sent those on board flying through the air like rag dolls, many landing lifeless in the shallow water. The Higgins boat had struck an underwater mine.

The shock wave from the blast knocked Alexander on his rear. After standing back up, he slogged through the bloody surf, pulling the wounded and the dead onto the beach. Then he continued his search for help for those on his damaged boat. But looking farther west along the beach and seeing the intensity of the fighting, he nixed the idea of seeking aid from that direction.

Frustrated and dejected, Alexander ran back to LCT 856, which was still smoking after the crew had snuffed out the fires. He and others tried to make the wounded as comfortable as possible. With what little supplies were on board, he gave them water, bandaged them, injected some with morphine, and offered words of encouragement. "We'll get you out of here soon," he told them. "I promise."

He helped move several bodies, including one that he had been stepping over several times. When he turned the corpse over, he shook his head in sadness. It was the just-married, newly commissioned executive officer Charlie Morgan. *I never had the chance to get to know him.*

Still keeping a lookout for help, Alexander spotted a lone Higgins boat about to drop off her passengers about 75 yards east of his LCT. *I've got to catch him before he pulls away.* Alexander leaped off his craft, ran down the beach, and then waded into the water, shouting and waving his arms. The Higgins boat started to back off but then stopped.

"You've got to help!" Alexander shouted. "I have about two dozen men badly wounded on my LCT over there. Please, you must save them."

The skipper of the Higgins boat shook his head and said, "My orders are to get out of here and bring in more troops."

"These men will die if you don't help," Alexander shouted.

"Just bring your boat along the port side of my craft and take them to a hospital ship. You're their only hope."

The skipper hemmed and hawed—should he follow his orders or his heart?—before he finally caved in to the ensign's pleas. Feeling immense relief, Alexander then helped transfer the wounded from the LCT to the Higgins boat, which then made it safely to a hospital ship. He also had ordered his surviving crewmembers to go with them.

Alexander chose to remain behind with several corpses that had been gently laid to one side of the craft. He was still trying to come to grips with the fate of his vessel when he noticed that the base of the cliff was getting crowded with wounded soldiers, who had crawled or stumbled there from other sections of Omaha Beach. The men were seeking protection that the cliff provided.

But Alexander knew they were in danger. *The tide is coming in and they'll soon be underwater.* He went over to a harried medic who was administrating to the wounded and said, "They can't stay here because they'll all drown if they do." Alexander pointed to a discolored line on the cliff, about six feet above the sand, and said, "That's the high-water mark from the incoming tide. We have to get them out of here."

"Where will we take them?" the medic asked. "We can't climb the cliff, and it's suicide if we go west of here."

"We'll bring them to my LCT. It's been destroyed but at least it's beached. There's nowhere else to go."

Alexander and the medic assisted the walking wounded and carried the others to the craft and lay them down on the hard steel deck, shoulder to shoulder, head to feet. Some whimpered, some cried, and one kept asking for his mother. Most, though, remained silent and somber.

Other than offer comforting words, there was little more that the exhausted ensign could do for them. The medical supplies on board the craft had already been used up from the earlier group of wounded sailors and soldiers. Alexander ordered that those who were in the worst shape spend the night in the damaged living quarters. Those who were not facing life-threatening injuries had to remain outside on the deck. When the high tide came in that night, the waves splashed over the bulkhead, soaking them.

Because much of the fighting had moved inland, the morning was calm on Fox Red. But the tide and current brought in countless bodies of Americans who had drowned or been killed before reaching shore. Alexander left the LCT in search of a radio operator to report his position and get aid for the wounded.

He was flabbergasted by the gruesome sight in front of him. Corpses littered a 50-yard swath of sand. He couldn't walk a straight line for four feet without having to step over or around a body. The devastated skipper refused to look at the faces out of fear that he would recognize a friend. *If I live to be a thousand years old, I will never forget this sight*, he thought.

He managed to get a landing craft to transport the wounded from his LCT to a hospital ship. Staying behind, he couldn't make contact with his unit and remained on the beach for five more days, sleeping in a foxhole.

He was finally able to catch a ride on a ship heading back to England. After hearing the ensign's story, an officer told him, "You have much to be proud of."

Replied Alexander, "We got most of our cargo ashore, battered but at a tremendously high price. I like to think that we distracted the enemy. I like to think that the time the enemy spent on pounding us with their eighty-eights was precious time our boys used to get a better hold on the beachhead. I like to think my little LCT did her part on a day that will go down in history."

Alexander, who was promoted to lieutenant, left the navy in 1947 and returned to his hometown of Indianapolis, where he and his wife, Mary, raised four sons and a daughter. He owned several businesses, including a group of Ace Hardware stores, before retiring in 1988.

In 2014, Alexander, a widower with 11 grandchildren, told the Indianapolis Star, *"All those years ago, and I still feel bad about those injured and killed on my boat. At the same time, I don't know what else I could have done. I was so dedicated to carrying out my orders."*

THE JUMPING CHAPLAIN

CAPTAIN FRANCIS SAMPSON

501st Parachute Infantry Regiment, 101st Airborne Division

Hände hoch!" ["Hands up!"] ordered two snarling Nazi soldiers.

Captain Francis Sampson complied and then let out an "oomph" when one of them jabbed a German submachine gun called a Schmeisser into his stomach. Sampson studied the badge pinned on each of their chests—a bird of prey with its talons clutching a swastika—and realized they were Hitler's *Fallschirmjäger*, hardcore, take-no-prisoners paratroopers.

Sampson tapped at the white cross painted on his helmet and then the tiny cross pinned to the collar of his fatigues. "I'm a Catholic priest, a chaplain," he said. Tugging at the brassard, a white cloth band with a red cross on it, high on his left arm, he added, "I'm a medic, too." He pointed to the farmhouse behind him and said, "It's full of wounded soldiers."

Whether or not the Germans understood him, they didn't care what he had to say. Besides, they had never seen an airborne chaplain before because their military didn't have any.

"*Hält die Klappe und bewege dich!*" ["Shut up and move!"] one of them commanded. They shoved the paratrooper-chaplain toward a road, stepped behind him, and prodded him in the back with their Schmeissers to keep him walking. *Where are they taking me?* he wondered. He hoped they would lead him to an officer who spoke English so Sampson could explain that the wounded Americans needed help. Wherever he was headed, he was somewhat relieved, thinking, *If they had wanted to shoot me, they would have done it already.*

After marching him about a quarter of a mile, the pair of Germans shouted, "*Hält!*" and pushed him up against a thick hedgerow. Then they stepped back and cocked their weapons.

They're going to kill me! Feeling his knees weakening and his throat tightening, he closed his eyes and began reciting the shortest prayer he knew. Then he heard the shots.

Sampson knew the risks of practicing his faith on the front lines. He had volunteered for this. Born in a small Iowa town, he wanted to become a Catholic priest from an early age. After graduating from Notre Dame University in 1937, he entered St. Paul's Seminary in Saint Paul, Minnesota. Ordained a priest for the diocese in Des Moines, Iowa, in 1941, he served in a parish in Neola, Iowa, and taught at Dowling High School in Des Moines.

Then the United States entered World War II. Sampson could have remained in Iowa, safe and secure, tending to his flock and students. But he felt a calling to serve his country, and, with permission from his bishop, entered the army as a chaplain. After finishing his training for the chaplaincy and earning a commission as a lieutenant, he learned the army was looking for chaplains for airborne units, so he volunteered.

He assumed chaplains wouldn't need to go through the paratroopers' incredibly rigorous training, but when he arrived at Fort Benning, Georgia, he discovered he was wrong. Just like every other trooper trainee, Sampson had to march double time for miles carrying a heavy backpack, conquer challenging obstacle courses, perform hours of demanding calisthenics, pass the physical fitness test, and, most important of all, learn how to jump out of airplanes. Sampson, a 30-year-old who stood 5 feet, 10 inches and weighed 185 pounds, had excelled at athletics in high school and college, but the airborne training sorely tested his physical capabilities. While many trainees washed out or landed in the hospital, he persevered and earned his coveted silver wings.

"Frankly, had I known of all this training and tortures of mind and body beforehand, I would've turned a deaf ear to the call for volunteers for airborne chaplains," he admitted to a fellow paratrooper.

"Why didn't you just quit?" Sampson was asked.

"Well, once I signed up, I was too proud to back out," he replied. "Besides, the airborne are the elite troops of the army, and I enjoy the prestige and glamour that goes with belonging to such an outfit."

In 1942, Sampson became the regimental chaplain for the 501st Parachute Infantry Regiment of the 101st Airborne

Division (a position he would hold throughout the war). Because of his compassion and sense of humor, he endeared himself to the men, who called him Father Sam. Promoted to captain, he qualified as a combat medic, having learned to apply a splint, infuse blood plasma, and perform other emergency first aid. Above all, he was a noncombatant who refused to carry a firearm, believing his weapon was his faith.

Naturally, one of his main priorities was meeting the spiritual needs of his men. On two English airfields in the days leading up to the Normandy invasion, he heard confessions from all the Catholics in the regiment. On the eve of departure, so many troops wanted to attend his Mass that he conducted two services and needed an hour to distribute communion. Talking to a fellow chaplain, who was a Protestant, Father Sam said, "When I write letters to the families of those men who die in combat, at least I can assure them that their sons had been well prepared for death."

For D-Day, more than 800 planes revved up their engines to transport more than 13,000 paratroopers, including 13 airborne chaplains. Before stepping into the C-47 that would drop him behind enemy lines, Father Sam checked his musette bag, a small backpack with a strap that contained his Mass kit. Inside, it held the items he needed to celebrate Mass wherever and whenever it was possible: a ciborium (a covered goblet-shaped vessel) to store consecrated communion wafers, a chalice, a crucifix, two candlesticks, and a daily missal (a book containing texts used in Masses throughout the year). It also contained cards with Latin texts for absolution and anointing the sick. He wrapped the objects in altar linens and his white priest vestments.

Like all men of the 101st, Father Sam was loaded with more than 100 pounds of extra gear, which, in his case, included medical supplies, blood plasma, a second musette bag of toiletries and underwear, and boxes of K rations. Also, in addition to his Mass kit, he carried a canteen of consecrated altar wine for Mass and another canteen of medical alcohol.

As each man boarded the plane, Father Sam shook his hand and said, "God bless you." While the aircraft taxied for takeoff, he offered up a simple prayer and then cracked a few jokes. The men chuckled out of politeness but once the plane lifted off, most everyone remained quiet. Although Father Sam looked calm, he wasn't. *No pair of knees are shaking more than mine, and no heart is beating faster,* he admitted to himself. *How many of us will survive to see tomorrow?*

When his plane neared its assigned drop zone shortly after 1 a.m., the Germans sent up heavy flak that buffeted the aircraft. Shrapnel pelted the fuselage, shooting up through the floor. One fragment pierced the plane's aluminum skin and lodged in a trooper's leg. After being treated for the wound, he insisted on jumping.

When it was his turn to make his first combat jump, Father Sam said under his breath, "I'm in your hands, O Lord." Then he leaped out into the darkness. Seeing flashes from enemy machine gun fire below and hearing comrades crying out in pain on the descent, the chaplain wondered, *How many of us will make it to the ground without getting shot up?*

Father Sam avoided the bullets but landed in a deep, flooded drainage ditch where his heavy gear dragged him under the water. Holding his breath, he pulled out his knife and, in a frantic effort to free himself, began furiously sawing on the straps that held his gear. Unable to see in the black water, he severed whatever items were in reach without concern for what he was jettisoning. When he removed enough gear, he was able to stick his head above water, but he still couldn't release himself from his parachute and its tangled lines.

While he continued to struggle, the canopy of his chute, which had stayed open on top of the surface, caught a stiff breeze and began towing him backward along the water-filled ditch. The wind yanked the chaplain for about 100 yards before he reached water shallow enough for him to dig in his heels and stop. Exhausted, he sat in the cold water until he regained his strength and wriggled out of his harness.

Whichever direction Father Sam looked, he saw yellow flashes from gun muzzles, orange streaks from tracer bullets, and bright bursts from antiaircraft fire. *It's like landing in the middle of a target range,* he thought. Scanning the immediate area, he hoped the moonlight would reveal nearby paratroopers, but he saw no one.

Determined to find the important items he had discarded—including medical supplies and especially his Mass kit—Father Sam crawled beside the ditch to the spot where he had landed.

Then he jumped in the water and felt around the bottom until he had to come up for air. During his foraging, he retrieved his medic's kit and other supplies. *I won't leave until I find my Mass kit,* he vowed. He tried repeatedly without success, but he refused to quit. Finally, on his sixth attempt, he located the kit. The discovery of its sacred contents comforted him, if only for a brief moment. During those few seconds, he forgot about his chilled, drenched body and the incessant enemy fire. *I found my Mass kit. Now I need to find my unit.*

He soon met up with his assistant, Private William "Buck" France, who also was soaking wet, having lost his rifle when he landed in a flooded field and nearly drowned. When they reached a hedgerow, they watched a C-47 that had been struck by antiaircraft fire spiraling out of control, its left wing engulfed in flames.

"It's heading straight toward us!" shouted Father Sam. The men buried their heads in the ground as the plane roared over them and crashed about 100 yards away, exploding into a huge orange fireball and flinging burning metal. When it was obvious that none of the men in the blazing wreckage had survived, the chaplain and his assistant prayed for the victims' souls. That was all they could do for the dead.

The two unarmed men worked their way across a marsh, where they encountered enemy fire. They ducked into a farmhouse and were surprised to see that its three rooms were crammed with about two dozen paratroopers who had been injured on landing or been shot. The casualties were receiving treatment from several medics, including Captain Tildon McGee, the Protestant chaplain for the 506th Parachute Infantry Regiment. He said that on his descent, he narrowly avoided plowing into a church steeple in Angoville-au-Plain. "Can you imagine the irony if I had?" he told Father Sam. "The headline would've read, 'Chaplain Killed by Church.'"

McGee said he had turned the farmhouse of Frenchman Théophile Fortin into an aid station for casualties coming from a savage battle for control of two nearby wooden bridges over the Douve River. The medics had run out of sulfa powder, so Father Sam and French used their supplies to help treat the men while the fight raged on outside.

Later in the day, an enemy mortar shell struck behind the house, killing the farmer's wife, Odette Fortin, and an eight-year-old girl, Georgette Revet, when the two were fetching water from the well. As Father Sam knelt to anoint them, Théophile Fortin threw himself on their bodies and broke out into agonizing sobs. The priest placed a hand on the shoulder of the grief-stricken man, but Fortin couldn't be consoled.

Inside the damaged aid station, McGee told Father Sam, "Some of our patients are getting worse. They need more help than we can give. They need a doctor."

"I'll find our regimental aid station and try to bring back a surgeon," Father Sam said. He then headed out on his own, trudging through a swamp that was sometimes chest deep to avoid the enemy. He eventually reached the village of

Basse-Addeville, where about 200 American GIs were engaged in a brutal firefight with a German unit a few hundred yards from the regiment's aid station, which was set up in an 18th-century stone house.

After hearing Father Sam's plea for help for the wounded under McGee's care, Major Francis Carrel, the regimental surgeon, sent his assistant surgeon and another medic along with supplies to the Fortin farmhouse. Father Sam chose to stay in Basse-Addeville to help treat the increasing number of wounded there.

But then Major Richard J. Allen, who was commanding the troops in the village, told Father Sam, "We've just received orders to pull out within the hour. Tell Doc Carrel that he, you, the medics, and the walking wounded are leaving with us. When we move, we have to go quickly because the Krauts will close in on this place fast. I'd like to stay and hold this position, but we don't have enough men to do it."

"But that means the wounded who can't walk will be left behind," Father Sam said.

Allen nodded. "It's a decision I hate to make, but for the safety of the whole unit, I have no choice."

When Father Sam relayed Allen's order, Carrel shook his head and said, "This is a bad time to leave them. The Germans aren't taking many prisoners now because they consider them a liability. I doubt anyone who stays here will survive."

"I'm staying with the wounded," Father Sam said. "It's my duty to be with them."

Carrel tried to talk him out of it, but the chaplain insisted on remaining behind with the 14 paratroopers who were too hurt to move. Carrel sighed and said, "I can't talk you out of your decision, but what I can do is give you a medic so you aren't alone with the wounded."

A sergeant tore a sheet of paper into six pieces—one for each of the medics at the aid station—and wrote the word "stay" on one of the slips. He folded all six pieces and tossed them in a helmet. Private Everett Fisher was the first medic to draw. He unfolded the slip. It said, "stay."

When Major Allen's forces left the village, Father Sam made a white surrender flag out of a bedsheet and hung it outside the door, hoping it would prevent the Germans from attacking the house. He expected them to show up within the hour, but all was quiet, so he sent Private Fisher out to scrounge for food. The medic returned with rations that had been abandoned during the fighting. He also brought bottles of wine and eggs from the pantry of an unoccupied house.

On into the night, Father Sam and Fisher cleaned wounds, changed dressings, and administered morphine to their patients. The chaplain spent much of his time with Technician 5th Grade Norman Dick, whose leg was nearly severed when a grenade in his pocket exploded after an enemy bullet struck it.

Father Sam gave him three units of plasma, trying to keep him alive. To help comfort Dick, who was a devout Presbyterian, the chaplain took a crucifix that was hanging on a wall in the house and gave it to him, and then helped him say his prayers.

Dick rallied, but shortly before 4 a.m., he faded. While still clutching the crucifix, he passed away in the chaplain's arms. Wishing they could have done more for him, Father Sam and Fisher gently rolled his body in a parachute and laid it outside.

Beginning at sunup, the chaplain went outside every 15 minutes and waved the makeshift surrender flag but didn't get any response. Later that morning, while making hot chocolate for the men, Father Sam gazed out the window and saw Germans setting up a machine gun in the front yard. It was aimed at the house. The chaplain ran out the front door, waving the white flag.

That's when he was confronted with two hostile German soldiers who stuck a Schmeisser in his belly and then marched him away from the house. After making him walk a few hundred yards, they told him to stop in front of a hedgerow. Then the soldiers stepped back and cocked their weapons.

Realizing he was about to be executed, Father Sam wanted to say the act of contrition, a short prayer expressing sorrow for one's sins. But he was so panicky that he unthinkingly recited the grace before meals: "Bless us, O Lord, for these and all Thy gifts, which of Thy bounty we are to receive through Christ Our Lord."

He closed his eyes as shots rang out. But they didn't come from the Schmeissers of the two soldiers. The shots were fired in the air by a German sergeant who was scurrying down the road, trying to get their attention. They lowered their weapons.

After talking to the soldiers, the sergeant spoke in broken English to Father Sam. Learning that the American was a Catholic priest, the sergeant snapped to attention, saluted, and bowed slightly. Then he pulled back the inside of his collar to reveal a pinned Sacred Heart, a Catholic medallion.

"We are of the same faith," said Father Sam. For the first time since he felt the muzzle of a Schmeisser poking him, he could breathe normally and relax his tensed muscles.

The sergeant escorted him to an intelligence officer who questioned him in fluent English. Explaining that he possessed no military information of value, the chaplain asked to return to his wounded men. The officer agreed and told the sergeant to escort the priest back to the aid station in Basse-Addeville.

When Father Sam entered the house, Fisher let out a joyful whoop. "When we heard the shots, we assumed the worst," the private said. "We thought for sure you were dead and that we would be massacred.

"Right after they took you away, three other German paratroopers kicked open the door and one of them stuck a pistol in my stomach and pulled the trigger. It clicked, and the boys on the floor had turned their backs, expecting me to get a belly full of lead. I showed my brassard, and he pulled his gun away. Then they shot up the ceiling to scare everyone and ransacked the house and took our food and filled their canteens with wine from a barrel in the shed out back."

The German sergeant made Father Sam show him the wounds of all the men and open all the drawers, cabinets, and cupboards to prove the Americans weren't hiding any weapons or ammunition. Once he was satisfied, the sergeant said, "I send doctor two, three days." Then he left, but the *Fallschirmjäger* dug foxholes and set up a perimeter that enclosed the aid station.

That night, the 101st Airborne Division tried to recapture Basse-Addeville with support from the 65th Armored Field Artillery Battalion, which began shelling the German position. Explosions rocked the stone farmhouse, showering the men in plaster dust when a ceiling beam cracked. Another blast blew out the windows and hurled stone, wood, and glass shards into the main room.

Father Sam and Private Fisher moved some of the wounded under the beds and braced the beds with drawers and furniture to protect the men from falling debris. For hours, the aid station had avoided a direct hit, although the shaking from nearby explosions caused the rafters to fall and even bandages to slip off the patients, who wailed in terror. Father Sam calmed them and led them in the Lord's Prayer.

Then three artillery shells crashed into the house, creating blinding blasts that knocked down the pantry's roof and walls. Instinctively, Father Sam threw himself over three men who were on the floor to protect them from what he expected would be the collapse of the entire house. But, amazingly, much of it remained standing.

Above the ringing in his ears from the explosions, the chaplain heard Corporal Elbert Yeager, a 23-year-old paratrooper from Texas, calling his name. Working his way through the debris, Father Sam found Yeager buried to his waist in the ruins of the pantry. "Father," he murmured, "they got me." The chaplain dropped to his knees, cradled Yeager's head in his lap, and prayed as the corporal took his final breath.

Hearing another groan from under the rubble, Father Sam dug through the debris to uncover paratrooper Sergeant Lowell Norwood. But by the time the chaplain had reached him, Norwood had died.

The concussions from the blasts had sent an army flashlight rolling out of the house and into the road. Somehow, the light was on, and the chaplain feared that US artillery observers might see it and use it as a target. Amid the continued shelling, he rushed outside and switched off the flashlight. Turning around, he saw a wounded German soldier writhing in pain in a ditch. Father Sam bent down to carry him into the aid station, but the man had perished.

The chaplain returned to the house just as another shell exploded near the doorway, causing more debris to fall. When a German soldier outside screamed for help, Father Sam stood up to assist him, but the wounded Americans begged him to remain inside for his own safety.

Before long, the Germans began to retreat as the advancing Americans entered the village. Not knowing that the stone farmhouse was an aid station, the GIs blasted it with rifle grenades and machine gun bullets. A red tracer bullet shattered a window, ricocheted off a wall, and nicked Father Sam's thigh, setting his pants on fire. He put out the flames but suffered second-degree burns on his blistered and bleeding thigh. After dressing his own painful wound, he went back to caring for the survivors.

When the Americans seized the village, they searched every building that was still standing. Holding a hand grenade, Lieutenant Sumpter Blackmon approached the stone farmhouse, unsure who, if anyone, was inside. Fisher saw Blackmon and shouted, "Americans are in here!" Father Sam limped out of the aid station and told Blackmon that 11 wounded paratroopers had survived the shelling.

Seeing the chaplain's charred, tattered pants and burned thigh, Blackmon asked, "What happened to your leg?"

"It's nothing," Father Sam replied. "Please, I need you to get these men out of here so they can receive the treatment they deserve."

Blackmon arranged for the evacuation in two jeeps that required three 10-mile round trips to a surgical facility established by the 101st at the Château de Colombières in Hiesville. Father Sam and Fisher helped carry the wounded, the most serious ones first, on stretchers to the jeeps. When the pair brought out Private Floyd Martin, who suffered bullet wounds to his face and shoulder, he glanced at the crumbled remains of the house and said, "I can't figure out how we ever came out of this alive."

Father Sam was the last in his group to arrive at the château, a stone building that looked like a medieval fortress. He, along with Captain Joseph Duehren, Catholic chaplain for the 401st Glider Infantry, carried in the wounded, wheeled them to the operating room, treated the less serious cases, and administered last rites to the dying.

About an hour after Father Sam arrived, he learned that a soldier with a bad abdominal wound and a rare blood type needed blood or he would die. The chaplain had Type O negative blood, the type that can be transfused to almost any patient, so he rolled up his sleeve and gave two pints for the GI.

Even though overworked Father Sam was sapped and drained, he sent Duehren to bed at 2:30 a.m. and carried on alone among the wounded, catnapping when he could. Barely able to remain on his feet, the chaplain toiled at the château until noon the following day when, under orders, he was taken to the village of Vierville. There, two paratroopers dug him a foxhole and stuffed it with a parachute for bedding. He lay down and slipped into such a deep sleep that he didn't wake up for 24 hours.

Days later, Father Sam arrived at a hospital attached to a convent and school a few miles from the city of Cherbourg. Although the complex had sustained serious damage, 50 nuns continued to treat more than 500 wounded combatants, including captured Germans. He pitched in to help administer aid and pray.

Wanting to find a good place to say Mass, Father Sam inspected the hospital's bombed-out chapel, where only a section of the roof and two walls remained. He was awed that one of the standing walls still held a life-size crucifix and that the statues of Saints Peter and Paul were intact. "It's a miracle," he marveled.

Later, in front of dozens of battle-weary men who packed into the ruined chapel, Father Sam celebrated Mass. In his homily (sermon), he said, "Hitler has tried to replace the image of our Blessed Lord on the cross with a stupid swastika . . . Nevertheless, like the bombs that were dropped on this chapel, they have only succeeded in making the cross stand out more and more in bold relief. The image we love grows greater in our understanding because of the [intensity] of the hate . . . in wicked men. Each of us has that sacred image stamped upon his soul . . . And no matter how we are torn by the bombs of tragedy . . . let us promise to shield forever His image in our hearts."

Father Sam was awarded the Distinguished Service Cross for his selfless help to the soldiers. The citation reads, in part, "The courage, fortitude, and heroism displayed by Chaplain Sampson are worthy . . . His intrepid actions, personal bravery, and zealous devotion to duty exemplify the highest traditions of the military . . . and reflect great credit upon himself, the 101st Airborne Division, and the United States Army."

For more than three weeks after D-Day, Father Sam remained in France, working under combat conditions with medics to rescue the wounded, offering Mass, hearing confessions, anointing the dying, and praying for the dead.

In September, he parachuted behind enemy lines into Holland with his airborne unit and set up an aid station that the Germans seized while he was at a command post. Three months later, during the Battle of the Bulge in Belgium, Father Sam learned that American paratroopers had been machine-gunned and left for dead on a nearby road. He took a jeep, hoping to retrieve them, but was captured by a German unit.

He and more than 1,500 POWs were marched in the bitter cold 185 miles through Luxembourg to Germany. On Christmas Eve, Father Sam led the men in prayer and song. He and his fellow prisoners were then herded into overcrowded boxcars on a six-day journey without food or water. They survived on only the snow scraped from the tops of the boxcars.

The survivors arrived at Stalag II-A, a prison camp that held about 25,000 Allied captives in northern Germany. Father Sam, who was the only Catholic priest among the 950 American POWs, turned down the Germans' offer to stay in the better quarters of the captured officers. Instead, he chose to be with the enlisted men. Under his direction, the men built a chapel in his barracks, where he held daily Mass and a nondenominational prayer service twice a week. After four months of harsh imprisonment, he rejoiced when Russian forces liberated the camp.

During the Korean War in 1950, Father Sam made his fourth and final combat jump. He remained in the military for nearly 30 years. Promoted to major general, he became the army's Chief of Chaplains from 1967 to 1971.

Shortly before he retired, Father Sam gave a speech in which he said, in part, "I have been asked how I can wear the uniform which symbolizes war and also wear the cross upon it symbolizing peace . . . I see nothing in this mission that does not appeal to the highest ideals of any man regardless of his religion. A great churchman once said if he had not been a priest, he most certainly would have been a soldier, because they are both called to the identical things: the preservation of peace, the establishment of justice when it has been lost, and the providing of security with protection for the weak and the innocent."

After brief stints as a parish priest, Father Sam lived out the rest of his life in Sioux Falls, South Dakota, where he died in 1996 at the age of 84.

Speaking about the role of faith in combat, General William Arnold, chief of staff of the army during World War II, once said, "Military power wins battles, but spiritual power wins wars."

MADNESS AND MAYHEM

ENSIGN JOSEPH "JOE" VAGHI, JR., AND HIS PLATOON
6th Naval Beach Battalion

Only a split second before he blacked out, Ensign Joe Vaghi heard that heart-stopping shrill whistle of an incoming artillery shell. The deafening noise from thousands of machine guns, M1 rifles, rocket launchers, mine explosions, and mortar rounds had cloaked the distinctive sound of the long-range shell until it was too late for Vaghi to react.

He and a member of his platoon had been ready to cart a wounded comrade out of harm's way on Omaha Beach when the blast threw him in the air and knocked him out even before he landed on his back in the sand.

A minute later, Vaghi opened his eyes, his mind muddled and his ears ringing and bleeding. *Where am I? What happened?* Staring up at the smoke-filled sky, he tried to gather his wits and understand why a burning sensation was spreading over his chest and legs. He sat up to take stock of himself and gasped. *My clothes are on fire!*

Grabbing handfuls of sand and spreading them over his smoldering pants and shirt, Vaghi smothered the flames.

He then scanned the immediate area and groaned. With their arms and legs spread in awkward positions, several wounded and unconscious men from his platoon were sprawled on the sand.

A few feet away from him, a jeep was burning, its front end consumed in flames. He recognized the vehicle. *Oh, my God, that's the jeep that's full of grenades! If the fire reaches them, we'll all be dead!*

He quickly weighed his options. He could try to drag all the casualties to a safe distance before the jeep blew up, or he could try to remove all the boxes of grenades before the flames ignited them. *I know what I have to do. But is there enough time to do it?*

The son of Italian immigrants, the Connecticut-born Vaghi was the third of nine children. (All six boys would serve in the US military during or immediately after the war—and all would make it home safely.) He worked in his father's cabinetry shop throughout his childhood and then attended Rhode Island's Providence College on a football scholarship, where he received a bachelor's degree in philosophy.

He wanted to become a pro football player, but the war changed his plans. Immediately after graduation in December 1942, Vaghi enlisted in the navy and completed an intensive 90-day midshipman training program at Notre Dame and was commissioned as a naval officer in April 1943. Chronic seasickness torpedoed his hopes of becoming a captain of a landing craft for amphibious assaults. Instead, the navy trained him as a beachmaster and assigned him to one of its beach battalions—units that arrived on shore in seaside invasions to establish and maintain a semblance of order.

The beachmaster was responsible for controlling the movement of troops, vehicles, supplies, and equipment on the beach and evacuating the wounded and dead. The job of his unit—the 6th Naval Beach Battalion—included clearing mines and blowing up obstructions to create paths for arriving troops, establishing radio communication with the ships at sea, arranging for medical aid and evacuation for injured personnel, guiding landing craft past submerged German obstacles, and providing temporary repairs of disabled boats during combat.

Put in charge of a platoon in Company C, Ensign Vaghi trained hard with his comrades in the United States for the D-Day invasion. In addition to learning about demolitions and first aid, the men of the beach battalion were required to handle every standard navy weapon from the .45-caliber Colt pistol to the large 5-inch cannon. Although they were sailors, they dressed as soldiers, wearing army fatigues, helmets, and para-trooper's boots, and carried rifles, carbines, and tommy guns.

Under the command of Eugene Carusi, the 400-member beach battalion arrived in England for final specialized training two months before the planned invasion. The unit was attached to the army's 5th and 6th Engineer Special Brigades and received orders through the army. For D-Day, plans called for the 6th Naval Beach Battalion to land on Omaha Beach with

Allied troops during the first two hours of the invasion. Vaghi's platoon would be responsible for Easy Red, a 250-yard-wide section of beach between the low- and high-water marks.

Even though the battalion was under the supervision of the army, it still remained a regularly commissioned navy unit—a fact that the naval supply system often overlooked. As an ignored military stepchild, the battalion never was issued important items such as foul-weather gear and other protective outerwear. The only way to obtain certain supplies was to beg, borrow, or steal things from navy warehouses—all with the approval of their commander—which earned the unit the nickname "Carusi and his 400 thieves."

During the crossing of the English Channel aboard the large landing craft LCI (L) 88, members of the battalion prepared themselves for the invasion in individual ways. Some prayed and read their Bibles. Others penned letters home, just in case they would be the last ones written. Several shared their fears with their comrades.

Coxswain Amin Isbir, who at age 36 was the oldest man in Vaghi's platoon, confided to the ensign, "I have a bad feeling about the invasion. I have a premonition that by the end of the day, I'll be dead."

"Don't think that way," Vaghi said. "It's going to be tough, sure. But you've trained for this moment, and you have to believe in yourself."

Isbir nodded. "I know I can do my job. But I have this strong feeling I won't get to complete it."

Vaghi patted him on the back and said, "Picture yourself returning home to McKeesport, Pennsylvania, a hero."

"I can. But I see myself in a coffin."

Other navy men were more confident, or at least they gave that impression based on their bluster and cheeriness. Vaghi chose to spend his pre-invasion hours doing what he enjoyed— playing cards. He joined Commander Carusi and several officers in the ship's wardroom for a game of "high, low, roll 'em," a distant cousin to poker. For chips, they used "funny money," the term for five-franc notes printed in America and issued to troops for use in France. The game went on until the wee hours of the morning, when it was time to prepare for the invasion.

Shortly after daybreak, Vaghi lined up his men as LCI (L) 88 made a beeline toward the heavily defended seaside cliffs, which navy destroyers were shelling. He tried to process the chaotic scene: Several small landing craft in the first assault wave were beached and burning, and bodies were floating in the water. Troops from other boats were wading in surf up to their necks through a deadly screen of tracer bullets. Vaghi knew that for every tracer bullet he saw, there were four more bullets that he couldn't see because every fifth bullet loaded in a German machine gun belt was a tracer.

An enemy artillery shell exploded a few yards off the starboard side, sending up spray that showered him and his men. *Easy Red isn't going to be so easy*, he thought.

As the ship cut through the waves, Vaghi recognized the landmark that he had seen from intelligence photos. *There's the house with the tower on top of the cliff. Good. We're heading right for our section of beach.* At 7:35 a.m.—1 hour and 5 minutes after the start of the invasion—the 88 grounded at low tide about 1,000 feet from the dune line.

"See, Amin?" Vaghi said to Isbir. "Smooth sailing all the way in. We're going to be fine."

Commander Carusi was first in line, waiting for the ramp to drop. Vaghi tapped him on the shoulder and said, "In case you forgot, last night when we were playing cards, we cut the deck to see who would go first. My queen beat your ten."

Carusi grinned and stepped back. "You can have the honor."

Before the men could leave, a crewman clad in only a helmet and swimsuit jumped off the bow while holding the man rope. Seconds after he plunged into the three-foot-deep water, an artillery round exploded directly in front of him, killing him instantly.

Vaghi didn't hesitate. He leaped off the ramp and charged toward shore as if he were back at Providence, running with the football through the defense. Alongside the 16th Infantry Regiment of the 1st Infantry Division, he and his platoon charged toward shore under heavy enemy fire.

Shortly after he left the 88, another artillery shell blew away the starboard ramp, killing two crewmen and injuring several troops on board and in the water.

Although Vaghi thought he was mentally prepared for combat, he was still surprised by the intensity of the enemy machine gun fire. Germans hunkered in their pillboxes and bunkers high above the beach on a bluff had an unobstructed view of the invaders and were slaughtering them.

The screeching overhead of 12-inch and 14-inch shells from the warships the USS *Texas* and the USS *Arkansas* offshore were sounds Vaghi had never heard before. The smell of expended gunpowder stung his nostrils as rocket launchers mounted on landing craft fired hundreds of rounds at a time into the German defenses. Purple smoke curled up from beach obstacles that the navy's demolition teams had blown up to clear a few paths.

Using the exposed obstructions in the shallow water as cover from enemy fire, Vaghi and his men hopscotched forward over the tidal flats. Then they raced more than 100 yards past countless dead and wounded until they made it to the dune line. When he saw that all members of his platoon, along with battalion commander Carusi, were still alive and combat fit, Vaghi boasted, "God is with us!" He winked at Isbir.

At age 23, Vaghi became the first and youngest beachmaster to step foot on the sands of Omaha. But he gave no thought to that distinction. Having reached the high-water mark, he and his men set about organizing themselves and planning their next move as they had done so many times during their training. The biggest difference between now and then was that they were pinned down by real machine gun fire.

Easy Red was becoming increasingly hectic. Several of the navy's demolition teams had been wiped out at the start of the invasion, so fewer gaps had been cleared of underwater obstacles leading into Omaha Beach. Because the teams had created an opening to Easy Red, more personnel and vehicles than planned came ashore on the section of beach under Vaghi's responsibility.

It quickly became so crowded that landing craft turned into sitting ducks for enemy fire. Assault tanks never made it to shore, having sunk or been blown up. Out in the bloody surf, boats that took direct hits were now pilotless, circling aimlessly with their dead, dying, and wounded troops.

Using flags, blinkers, and a powered megaphone, Vaghi began directing troops, vehicles, and supplies here, there, and everywhere.

"Beachmaster!" an army officer yelled at Vaghi. Pointing to a group of frightened soldiers who were cowering behind several obstacles, the officer ordered the ensign, "Get on your megaphone and tell those soldiers to get off the beach and move forward!"

Moments after Vaghi relayed the order, an army sergeant brought over a Bangalore torpedo, an explosive charge on the end of an extendable pole. He pushed it through a mass of barbed wire that the Germans had strung on top of a dune and exploded the obstacle, opening an exit off the beach. The sergeant then turned to his men and yelled, "Follow me!" He led the way, and they rushed through the gap to the base of the bluff about 50 yards away. But because the area was heavily mined, several soldiers were blown up. That didn't stop the troops. They poured through the opening and fanned out to attack German strong points.

Some members of the beach battalion plucked rifles from the sand and joined soldiers in assaults of pillboxes and machine gun nests. Others in heavy machinery continued clearing paths of obstacles and mines on the beach for troops to advance.

The units' medical teams set up aid stations and began treating casualties. Whenever he could, Vaghi pitched in to help, but he couldn't always tell the living from the dead. Because many injured troops lying at the water's edge were drowning from the rising tide, his men tried to drag them to safety only to end up casualties themselves. So many incoming troops were wounded and in need of treatment that Vaghi's men began scavenging medical supplies from the dead. Hoping to stem the carnage, Carusi ordered a temporary halt to the landings at 8:30 a.m. (Not until 11:30 a.m. did battle conditions improve enough for the beach battalions to begin evacuation of casualties to waiting hospital ships.)

Corpsman Frank Walden and 16-year-old hospital apprentice Virgil Mounts, who was the platoon's youngest member, were tending to the wounded behind the shingle, which provided limited safety.

When two army stretcher bearers carrying a casualty were hit by shrapnel from an explosion, Walden and Mounts raced to their aid. While the pair was treating them, an artillery shell landed and exploded a few yards away. Flying shrapnel ripped completely through Mounts and struck Walden in the left arm, leg, and side. Mounts died instantly but Walden was still alive.

Signalman Richard "Red" Onines, who temporarily lost his hearing from the blast, leaped up from behind the shingle, threw Walden over his shoulder, and hauled him to safety. Then Onines sprinted back to the impact area and brought out hospital apprentice Don Burrows, who also was seriously injured in the explosion.

At the first aid station, a pain-wracked Walden mumbled a thank-you to Onines and asked, "What . . . about . . . Virgil?"

"He's dead, Frank," Onines replied. "In a way, he saved your life. I saw shrapnel pieces pass right through his body and end up in you. If he hadn't taken the hits, those fragments would have killed you."

Meanwhile, the men who handled the platoon's communications were continuing to radio Vaghi's reports of battlefield conditions and supply needs to a control vessel offshore. What no one knew at the time was that the Germans had zeroed in on the platoon's radio frequency and pinpointed its location. As soon as the enemy had the coordinates, a German long gun on the back of a flatbed railroad car was rolled into position to fire.

Back on the beach, Vaghi noticed a wounded soldier had been left alone on a stretcher in the line of fire. The ensign shouted to Isbir, "Come help me! We need to get him to the first aid station ASAP!"

In the noise of combat, Vaghi and Isbir couldn't hear the screeching sound of the artillery shell fired by the German long gun. They were not aware it was heading straight for them. While Vaghi was on his knees gripping one end of the stretcher, Isbir had just arrived and was bending over when the round exploded a few feet away.

Vaghi lost consciousness for about a minute. The explosion had set his clothes on fire, but he managed to snuff out the flames before they charred his skin. Only a few feet away from Vaghi was an overturned jeep. He had no recollection of being that close to it before the blast. Within a short radius of the shell crater lay several of his men, some unconscious and others wounded or stunned.

Nearby, another jeep—one he knew carried two five-gallon cans of gasoline and boxes of hand grenades—was burning. The flames were working their way from the front of the vehicle toward the back. He had recovered sufficiently to understand that if the fire set off the grenades, he and everyone else around him likely would perish.

Vaghi staggered to his feet and felt an excruciating pain in his left knee, which was bleeding after being struck by hot shrapnel. He limped toward the burning jeep. Seeing platoon corpsman Bob Millican, who was shakily getting up, Vaghi yelled, "Bob, come with me! We must get the grenades out of the jeep before they blow up!"

The two of them lurched to the vehicle where, only three feet away, lay the platoon's 19-year-old radio operator, Torre

Tobiassen. Millican's instinct as a medic was to pull Tobiassen away from the burning jeep, but Vaghi stopped him. "There's no time for that! The only way to save him and the others is to get the grenades away from the flames."

The two began pulling out the boxes and tossing them a safe distance from danger. Vaghi could feel the heat from the flames growing hotter as they advanced toward the grenades. "Faster! Faster!" he shouted to Millican. They hauled out the last of the boxes and the two full gas cans just as the fire reached the back end of the vehicle.

Then the pair dragged Tobiassen away from the fire and revived him. While Millican went to treat other casualties felled by the explosion, Vaghi hobbled off to carry out his many duties as beachmaster.

Shortly afterward, he learned the full extent of the toll from the artillery shell that had knocked him out. Several of his men had received major and minor wounds. But under the overturned jeep, they found the body of Amin Isbir. "The explosion tossed the jeep in the air and it landed right on top of him," reported one of the men. "He never knew what hit him."

Vaghi bowed his head, sighed, and said, "Amin told me during the crossing he had a premonition that he wouldn't make it out of here alive. It's sad knowing he was right."

There was no time to mourn the loss; the ensign had too much to do. He and surviving members of the beach battalion continued to supervise the constant back and forth of landing craft that were delivering supplies and departing with the wounded and the dead.

At one point during the day, Ed Gallogly, a former classmate of his at Providence College who was now a navy lieutenant, came ashore and ran into Vaghi. Even though the enemy was firing at new arrivals, Gallogly took a moment to shout, "Hi, Joe! What are you doing here?"

Vaghi grinned for the first time since the start of the invasion and replied, "Just out for a stroll on the beach."

Seeing an unattended army bulldozer about 30 yards from the high-water mark, Vaghi thought, *I need to get that dozer off the beach area before it gets shelled.* He had no idea how to operate one, but it had always been a childhood dream to drive one. Grunting from the pain in his knee, he climbed on and, after a few seconds of study, started it up and began maneuvering it to a safer location.

He had traveled only 15 feet when one of the men from the beach brigade, Clyde Whirty, ran up to him and shouted, "Commander Carusi wants you off the dozer. He says you're more valuable as a beachmaster than as a bulldozer operator."

Vaghi knew that Carusi was right. "Perhaps another time," Vaghi sighed as he got off.

Whirty, an experienced heavy-machine operator even though he was only 19 years old, took his place, ready to clear paths on the beach of enemy obstacles and wreckage. "Today's my birthday," Whirty said. "Ain't that somethin'?"

The day before the invasion, Whirty was behind the controls of a bulldozer that was ready for loading onto an LCM (landing craft, mechanical), a vessel designed to carry large vehicles and machinery onto or close to shore. But the loading hit a snag. The dozer couldn't fit on the LCM because the blade was too wide. After a frantic search for a torch, workers removed a foot off each end of the blade of Whirty's dozer and others as well.

While Whirty waited for the completion of the job, England's royal couple, King George VI and Queen Elizabeth, showed up at the dock to offer encouragement to the men and pass out American flags as a show of support for the troops. The queen—who Adolf Hitler declared was the "most dangerous woman in Europe"—personally handed Whirty a flag, which he promptly secured to his dozer.

The next day, early in the invasion, he drove his bulldozer—with its Stars and Stripes flapping in the wind—off the LCM. But before he reached the beach, he struck a mine. The blast disabled the machine and slightly wounded the bigboned teenager.

He grabbed the flag, jumped off the wreck, and waded over to another bulldozer, whose driver had been shot in the head. After Whirty climbed on, he shoved the body off and drove the dozer onto the beach, but he was stopped by a mortar round that disabled the machine. Miraculously, the round didn't explode, sparing Whirty from death.

Taking the flag with him once again, he hopped down and

went looking for another bulldozer to operate. That's when he ran into Commander Carusi, who ordered him to take over the dozer that Vaghi had been driving.

Before operating the third dozer, Whirty fastened the flag behind his seat. Then he began clearing paths. What bothered him the most was moving bodies out of the way for trucks and jeeps to pass.

Incensed by the sight of Whirty's Old Glory, the Germans kept shooting at his bulldozer until the bullets eventually knocked it out of commission.

Whirty found a fourth unattended bulldozer. As the young navy man was attaching the flag to it, Vaghi came over and ordered, "Stow that flag, Clyde. Can't you see it's drawing fire? You aren't any good to us if you're shot full of holes."

"Understood," Whirty said. But as soon as Vaghi headed off, the teen ignored the order. He secured the Stars and Stripes and continued on his assigned mission—while adding one of his own. Whenever he saw a group of American soldiers pinned down, he would deliberately draw enemy fire away from them so they could advance. Incredibly, he avoided getting shot.

By the end of the day, his flag had been riddled with bullets, but it was still proudly flying.

Three of the nine beachmasters in the 6th Naval Beach Battalion perished on D-Day, and a fourth died the next day. For more than half a century, the navy barely acknowledged the battalion's existence and failed to honor its service at Normandy. It wasn't until

2000 that the battalion finally received the recognition it deserved when the navy gave it a Presidential Unit Citation.

For removing the boxes of grenades from the burning jeep on D-Day, Vaghi was awarded the Bronze Star. According to the citation, "This act involving utter disregard of personal safety unquestionably resulted in saving the lives of a number of wounded men who were immediately adjacent to the jeep." More than 80 members of the unit received the Bronze Star, including Bob Millican and Frank Walden.

After 23 days in Normandy, Vaghi returned to the United States to train navy officers in amphibious warfare. He then shipped out for the Pacific, where he served as a division officer of the landing team that invaded Okinawa. Discharged from the navy in 1947 with the rank of lieutenant commander, he remained in the naval reserve until 1959.

The knee injury he sustained on D-Day prevented him from attempting a career in pro football. Instead, he attended Catholic University and, after earning a degree in architecture, founded an architecture firm in Bethesda, Maryland, which he headed for more than four decades. In addition to his work in the Washington area, where he specialized in the restoration of old buildings, he was a consultant for the National World War II Museum in New Orleans. He and his wife, Agnes, raised four sons and had six grandchildren.

In 1995, Vaghi accompanied President Bill Clinton and Vice President Al Gore to Normandy to mark the 50th anniversary of V-E Day (Victory in Europe Day). He went there again in 2001 as the leader of a group of veterans who placed a plaque in honor of the 6th Naval Beach Battalion.

In a ceremony in 2012 at the French Embassy in Washington, Vaghi and 20 other World War II veterans were presented the Legion of Honor Chevalier—France's highest civilian award—for their personal, heroic contributions to the liberation of France during World War II. A few months after the ceremony, Vaghi passed away. He was 92.

BEYOND THE
CALL OF DUTY

SERGEANT WALTER EHLERS
Company L, 18th Infantry Regiment, 3rd Infantry Division

After a hard day toiling in the fields on the family farm, 18-year-old Walter Ehlers guzzled water from a hand pump and then plunked down on a rocking chair next to his grandfather on the front porch. "Walter," said the old farmer, "Germany is gonna be startin' another war real soon."

"What makes you say that, Grandpa?"

"The Nazis are burnin' books and takin' children away from their families and puttin' them into government schools for brainwashin'. Those Nazis are confiscatin' guns from private citizens. Yep, there's gonna be a war."

It was June 1939, and Walter had just finished high school in Junction City, Kansas. At the time, war was something he read about in history class. But Grandpa was a smart, perceptive man who could read, write, and speak German. He based his prediction after listening to newscasts on the radio and receiving letters from cousins who were living in Germany.

"I just hope you never have to experience combat," Grandpa said, "'cause sure as shootin', America is gonna get dragged into a humdinger of a war. You wait and see."

Less than three months later, on September 1, Germany invaded Poland, igniting World War II. Heeding Grandpa's warning that the US would soon enter the fray, Walter's older brother Roland decided to enlist rather than wait to be drafted. "If you're enlisting, then I am, too," Walter told Roland.

In October 1940, the brothers went to nearby Fort Riley. An army recruiter welcomed Roland, 23, but told Walter, 19, "You're too young to sign up on your own. You need your parents' signatures."

When Walter asked his parents, his father, John, agreed but his mother, Marie, hesitated. "I'll sign only if you promise me that you'll be a good Christian soldier," she told him.

"I'll do my best not to dishonor you or God," he replied.

After his parents signed the papers, he joined Roland in basic training in California. But Walter spent a lot of time thinking about his faith. *What am I doing here?* he asked himself. *I didn't come here to learn how to kill people.* He considered becoming a conscientious objector, a person opposed to serving as a combatant in the military for moral or religious reasons. But after further soul-searching, he realized he could practice his faith and be an effective soldier. *It's my duty to fight the enemy. The US has fought for freedom since the Revolutionary War, and part of that freedom is practicing the religion of your choice.*

After reaching that conclusion, he trained for battle like he did for his high school football team. To get in top physical shape, he did extra calisthenics and carried heavier loads than other trainees. He also became an expert shot with his M1 rifle.

Shortly after the US entered the war, Walter's other brother, Claus, who was two years older, was drafted and sent to fight in the South Pacific.

In November 1942, Walter and Roland, who had trained together in the same infantry unit, prepared in North Africa for their first taste of combat. From his backpack, Walter took out a photo of their mother. It wasn't the most flattering picture of her because she wasn't smiling. "She's probably not too happy right now with her boys at war," Walter told his brother.

"Maybe so," Roland replied. "But she's mighty proud of us."

Days later, as their landing craft rocked and rolled toward the Moroccan coast in the Allied invasion of Casablanca, Walter turned green and struggled to keep from vomiting.

"Nervous?" Roland asked.

Walter nodded and moaned, "Yes, and I'm seasick, too— very seasick. I wish the enemy would just blow my head off right now and put me out of my misery."

Roland laughed and said, "You'll forget all about it once we hit the beach." When the landing craft reached the shore, he told Walter, "See you later today after we take care of business." He said it so matter-of-factly as if he were talking about baling hay on Grandpa's farm. Walter, who always looked up to Roland, felt a surge of confidence in his brother's words. "Yeah," said Walter. "See you in a few hours."

Walter high-stepped through the surf, forgetting all about his seasickness and nervousness just as Roland had said. But when Walter made it to the beach, he froze and gasped. A fellow soldier lay dead in the sand. Walter had never seen a corpse before in real life. He began running again after he heard his brother shout, "Walter, move, move, move!"

Walter never hesitated in combat again, although before every battle, he often threw up from a nervous stomach. After the capture of Casablanca, the brothers were transferred to Company K of the 18th Infantry Regiment, 3rd Infantry Division, where they honed their fighting skills in several skirmishes with the enemy. During the Battle of El Guettar, in Tunisia, the unit was low on ammo but still withstood a withering German attack. Time and again, Walter impressed his superiors with his battlefield courage and competence.

The brothers made a pact with each other that if one fell during battle, the other would not stop to help him but would keep fighting because the whole unit needed to advance. "We keep on goin'," Roland told Walter. "Agreed?"

Walter nodded, shook Roland's hand, and said, "Agreed."

A year later, in 1943, the brothers took part in the invasion of Sicily. Early in the assault, an artillery shell landed near Roland, burying him in debris. Roland, who was dug out by his fellow soldiers, suffered severe shrapnel wounds to his back and was evacuated to a hospital. He didn't reunite with Walter until six months later, in Dorchester, England, where their unit was training for D-Day.

In March 1944, the company commander summoned the Ehlers brothers into his office and said, "I have some important things to tell you. We'll be fighting in a heavily defended area in France, so you should increase your GI insurance coverage to the maximum ten thousand dollars. It's going to be very dangerous, and there's only a fifty-fifty chance that both of you will survive. That's why I have to split you up. Army policy doesn't want brothers in the same unit in combat. It lessens the likelihood that both of you will be killed, so your parents won't suffer twice the heartache."

Walter was transferred to L Company, but the brothers still saw each other most evenings. Promoted to staff sergeant, Walter was put in charge of a squad of goof-offs, goldbrickers, and greenhorns who had plenty of experience playing music, but none shooting at the enemy. The fun-loving group included a singer and guys who played the guitar, violin, accordion, ukulele, or banjo. They were much better musicians than they were soldiers, having repeatedly failed inspections because they didn't care about polished boots and tight sheets.

"If we don't pass inspection, we won't get any leave," Ehlers told them. "And if I don't go on leave because of you clowns, I'll make so much trouble for you that combat will seem like a walk in the park." Within a few weeks, he whipped them in shape, earned their respect, and helped them pass every inspection.

One day the brothers were given passes to visit London, which had been ravaged by years of German bombing runs. The pair was shocked at the massive destruction. "Seeing block after block after block destroyed, it's hard to believe people continue to live here," Walter said.

That night, while the brothers were having dinner, air raid sirens blared—the signal for everyone to rush to the nearest bomb shelter. Walter and Roland followed a group of Londoners into a subway tunnel, where people sat on benches and waited out another enemy attack. Explosions rocked the shelter, showering the occupants with dust and plaster.

"We're trapped and there's nowhere else to hide," Walter whispered to Roland. "What if it caves in? We'll be buried alive." Walter didn't need to ask his big brother if he was scared. Walter could tell by the way Roland was tapping his foot. *Yeah, he's as scared as I am.*

"I'd rather take my chances fighting in combat than be stuck down here," Roland said. "And if I die before my time, I sure don't want to be buried in foreign soil."

When Walter studied the expressions of the Londoners in the shelter, he noticed they looked weary, but also calm and stoic as if they had grown used to three years of relentless bombing. No one was crying. No one was trembling. After the raid ended and the "all clear" sounded, the Londoners left the shelter and went about their business. Admiring their resolve, Walter said, "They're amazing. They carry on with their daily lives as if getting bombed is just a mere annoyance."

On the night before D-Day, the brothers said their good-byes. "There's no need to worry about each other," Roland said. "We each have our own responsibilities to deal with." After wishing each other luck, he told Walter, "We'll meet up on the beach." They bear-hugged and boarded their respective ships.

Walter's squad was supposed to come ashore in the second assault wave, but because so many troops had been killed or wounded in the first wave, more men were needed immediately. So at 8 a.m., two hours before the rest of his company hit the sand, Ehlers and his 12-man squad were ordered onto a landing craft for Omaha Beach. Their mission: fight their way five miles inland and scout the German-held town of Trévières.

As their vessel aimed toward the beach, his squad looked alarmed at the noise and the chaos. "Follow me, and do as I say," Ehlers told the men moments before their landing craft unloaded them onto a sandbar about 100 yards offshore.

When he jumped in, the water was up to his neck. His second-in-command was shorter and slipped under the surface. Ehlers, who was 6-foot-1 and weighed 165 pounds, grabbed him by the collar and kept his head above water until it was shallow. When the squad reached the beach, bodies and limbs were scattered along the shoreline. Troops squeezed behind obstacles, pinned down by German machine guns.

Seeing his men trying to dig in on the beach rather than advancing, Ehlers shouted, "We can't stop here! That's a sure-fire way of getting killed! We have to get off this beach!"

Running through a torrent of bullets spewing from two pillboxes, Ehlers led the squad past other troops who were staying put, wounded, or dead. When he and his men reached a relatively safe spot near the back of the beach, he flashed a grin. No one had suffered a scratch.

"I can't believe it," said the banjo player. "I thought for sure we'd all be dead by now." Others nodded in agreement.

"Just stick with me and do as I say," Ehlers told them. "I'll do my darnedest to keep you safe."

A beachmaster motioned the squad toward a hill, telling Ehlers, "Just follow the path that our boys have cleared of land mines. Don't stray from it. See what happens if you do?" He pointed to the bodies of several troops who had stepped to their deaths.

Even though bullets were streaming from pillboxes, the squad slipped through blown openings in two rows of barbed wire obstacles. When Ehlers and his men neared the hilltop, they came upon two demolition-team soldiers, each one carrying a Bangalore torpedo. They couldn't reach a third barbed wire barricade ahead of them because of enemy fire.

"We can't move forward until the wire is blown," Ehlers told them. "We'll provide cover fire so you boys can clear a path for us." While the squad kept up a barrage on the German positions, the two demo men sprinted toward the barricade.

Enemy bullets felled one of them, but the other was able to blow a hole in the wire large enough for Ehlers and his squad to run through.

He led a charge to the hilltop, and then he and his men jumped into a trench, where they surprised a German squad. During a brief firefight, several Germans ran off or were killed, but four surrendered. Ehlers had two men escort the captives to a command post for interrogation. Meanwhile, one of the pillboxes on the bluff continued to lay down overwhelming fire on the beach below. Trying to silence it, a soldier from another unit ran toward it while carrying a satchel charge (an explosive). But before he could get close enough to toss it into the structure, he was gunned down.

"We have to knock it out of action," Ehlers told his men. "Boys, cover me. Just keep pouring lead into the pillbox. I'll do the rest." While they riddled the pillbox, Ehlers sneaked up from the right flank, then stepped in front and killed the machine gun crew with a rapid-fire burst from his M1.

For the next six hours, he led his men against heavily defended enemy positions, constantly exposing himself to hostile fire, including once when a bullet creased his helmet. Even though it was common practice for a squad leader to remain in the back and have a rifleman act as point man, Ehlers always went first because he had the experience. Once, when the guitar player worried that Ehlers was taking too many risks, Ehlers replied, "I know what I'm doing. What's worse than me getting killed is getting all of you killed."

Slowly but steadily, he and his men advanced from hedgerow to hedgerow until they ran into a much larger German force. The Americans held their ground for several hours, even though enemy planes strafed the area and artillery shells exploded around them.

When the rest of his company finally showed up and routed the Germans from their initial defensive positions, Ehlers looked for his brother but couldn't find him. Talking to the men of Roland's platoon, he learned that Roland was missing in action. No one had seen him on the beach. The news—or lack of it—weighed heavily on Walter, but he forced himself to stay focused on the invasion. *That's what Roland would want,* he thought.

That night, Walter and several comrades tailed a German patrol that had unwittingly trekked through the company's perimeter. During a brief skirmish, the Germans ran off, but one of them was wounded and dropped a satchel, which Ehlers recovered. Inside were maps for the enemy's second and third lines of defense.

The next day, as the fighting moved inland, Ehlers and his squad—still intact without any serious injuries—worked tirelessly and efficiently at pushing the Germans out of their fortifications among thickets, hedgerows, and farmhouses. At one point, the squad was leading the platoon when the Germans counterattacked. Ehlers and his men sprinted for the safety of a hedgerow. While waiting to see if the enemy would try to creep up on them, Ehlers sniffed the air. "I can smell them," he whispered to his men, explaining that the German soldiers drank a dark ale that left an odor on their bodies when they sweated. "They're on the other side of the hedgerow."

In stealth mode, he walked along the thick hedgerow. When he slipped through an opening between the trees, he came face-to-face with a four-man German patrol. Before they could pull the trigger, he fired his M1, killing all of them. When his squad joined him and saw what he had done, Ehlers reloaded his weapon and said, "I didn't have time to argue with them."

Spotting a machine gun nest that was firing on one of the company's platoons, Ehlers slinked up on it from the side and killed the three-man crew. About 100 yards away, four enemy soldiers were firing a .30-caliber machine gun at another platoon. Once again, Ehlers sneaked up on the nest, this time from behind, and took out the entire crew.

Knowing the immediate area was teeming with Germans, he wanted his men to attach their bayonets to the barrels of their rifles, so he ordered, "Fix bayonets!"

"Does that mean we're going into hand-to-hand combat?" asked the accordion player.

"Let's hope not," Ehlers replied. "Bayonets have a strong psychological effect on the Germans. They fear them, so that gives us the advantage if we have to charge them."

Minutes later, while leading his squad, he caught a glimpse of three 80mm mortars manned by several Germans who were firing at the Americans from a depression in the ground. With his men right behind him, Ehlers ran up to the edge that over-looked the enemy position and yelled, *"Hände hoch! Kapitulieren!"* ["Hands up! Surrender!"]

Instead of giving up, they reached for their sidearms. Ehlers began shooting. So, too, did the rest of his squad. When the surviving Germans saw the bayonets on the Americans' rifles, they tried to flee, but the squad shot them. "They had their chance to surrender, and they made the wrong decision," Ehlers told his men. "We had to shoot them now or else we would be fighting them again later."

While he and his squad kept moving deeper into enemy territory, they discovered another manned machine gun nest and wiped it out. When his men stopped for a breather, Ehlers told them, "Three machine gun nests and a mortar section. Not bad for a morning's work."

During the break, his thoughts drifted toward his brother. *I have to believe Roland is still alive*, he told himself. *There's no reason to think otherwise.* From his backpack, he took out the photo of their mother, stared at it, and, as if talking to her, said, "I'll find Roland. He'll be okay."

The next morning, Ehlers and his squad were once again at the forefront of the entire platoon, which was the spearhead of the company. Within the hour, the platoon was so far ahead of the rest of the company that it suddenly found itself nearly surrounded, taking fire from the front and both flanks.

"Fall back!" the company commander ordered the platoon.

"Ehlers, you and your squad cover the withdrawal! Everyone else, fall back!"

The squad valiantly stood its ground until the rest of the company had retreated. But Ehlers knew it would be difficult for him and his men to withdraw from an enemy that was so close. *If we turn tail and run, we'll all get shot in the back*, Ehlers thought. *I need to draw fire away from my men.*

He charged to the top of a mound and started shooting toward his left flank, where the heaviest enemy fire had been coming from. He was joined by Corporal Jake Pearson*, a squad member who wielded a Browning automatic rifle (known as a BAR), the only fully automatic weapon in the squad. Standing side by side, they fired in a semicircle to keep the Germans from shooting at the retreating squad. The two of them provided cover long enough for their comrades to withdraw behind a hedgerow.

As the pair was ready to fall back, Ehlers spied three Germans setting up a machine gun aimed at the hedgerow where the squad had sought cover. Ehlers opened fire on the Germans, killing all three.

But then shots rang out from a different direction. "Sniper!" Ehlers shouted, just as a bullet struck him, spinning him around. The round had entered just below his right shoulder blade, traveled through his chest, bounced off a rib, and then exited his back near the entry wound. As he began falling on his back, he sighted the sniper and fired. The sniper tumbled out of a hedgerow, hitting the ground almost the same time as Ehlers did.

Before he was killed, however, the sniper had shot Pearson in the right arm, leg, and wrist. Pearson had collapsed in a bloody, unconscious heap. His BAR lay several feet away in the open.

While on the ground, Ehlers made a quick assessment of his own injuries. He moved his arms and legs. *Whew, they're okay.* Despite the growing pain on his right side, he crawled over to his rifleman, who had regained consciousness.

As enemy bullets glanced off rocks next to them, Ehlers said, "Let's get out of here!"

Pearson muttered, "I'm hit bad. I can't walk."

Still holding his M1, Ehlers put his left arm under his comrade's left arm and struggled to pick him up. Then as he helped drag him away, Ehlers continued to fire with his free hand, his right one, even though his right side was bleeding badly.

After getting the soldier to the safety of the hedgerow, Ehlers called for a medic, who came running and began working on Pearson.

Seeing the BAR on the mound, Ehlers thought, *If we have any chance at holding off the Germans, we're going to need that gun.* Forgetting about his own wounds, he wobbled back to the mound and crawled into the open. While firing his M1 with his right hand, he retrieved the BAR with the other. Then he slipped back down the mound, avoiding enemy fire.

When he returned to his squad, they were loading Pearson into an ambulance. "Great job getting the BAR," the company commander told Ehlers.

"Thanks, sir. Mind if the medic looks at me?"

"You've been shot?"

"Yes, sir, in the back."

"Let me look."

Ehlers turned around and raised his shirt so the officer could see the bullet wounds on his side. "My God, Ehlers, you've been shot clear through!" the officer exclaimed. "You should be dead!"

"Well, I'm still alive and kicking," Ehlers replied with a half grimace and half grin.

While examining the wounds, the medic told Ehlers, "This is pretty bad. You need to get in the ambulance."

"Nope," Ehlers replied. "What I need is to be with my men. Somebody has to lead and protect them. Just patch me up, Doc, and I'll go on my way."

After getting bandaged, he gripped his M1, slung a bandolier of eight clips over his good shoulder, and rejoined his squad. It was too painful for Ehlers to carry his backpack so he tossed it in a jeep.

Later that evening, during a lull in the fighting, Ehlers retrieved his backpack. While going through it, he discovered the full path of the bullet that struck him. It had exited his back, pierced his backpack, bored through a bar of soap, torn a corner off his mother's photo, and then became embedded in the trench shovel attached to his pack.

Showing his fellow soldiers the bullet's path and the nicked picture, Ehlers said, "See that stern look on my mother's face? She's saying, 'How dare they!'"

Five weeks later, the company commander found Ehlers and told him that Roland was dead. He had been killed instantly on Omaha Beach on D-Day when a mortar round struck his landing craft just as he was running down the ramp. After his body had been identified, it was buried near the beach.

Recalled Ehlers in a 2003 interview, "When I got the news, I was devastated. I found a private place and then for the only time during the war, I went to pieces. Roland was the bravest man I ever knew. He was my hero, always looking out for me. Not a day goes by that I don't think about him."

In keeping with Roland's wishes not to remain in foreign soil, his body was exhumed and transported back to the United States, where he was buried in Manhattan, Kansas. Their other brother, Claus, who fought in the South Pacific, survived the war and raised a family in Indiana, where he worked for a company that made musical instruments.

During the fight across France, Ehlers, who was promoted to staff sergeant, suffered a severe shrapnel wound in his left thigh in the town of Saint-Lô. After being hospitalized, he rejoined his unit at the Hürtgen Forest in Germany where he was wounded again, this time in the right leg and both shoulders. Following another hospitalization, he took over command of a platoon at the Battle of the Bulge in Belgium and was wounded in the right leg. In a 2012 interview for WWII Magazine, he said of his last wound, "I've still got the bullet in there. The Germans didn't leave much of me untouched."

For his actions on D-Day and the immediate days afterward, Ehlers received the Medal of Honor in December 1944. According to the citation, "The intrepid leadership, indomitable courage, and fearless aggressiveness displayed by Staff Sergeant Ehlers in the face of overwhelming enemy forces serve as an inspiration to others."

After the war, Ehlers settled in Buena Park, California, where he raised a family and worked as a benefits counselor for the Veterans Administration. Ehlers, who was invited to every presidential inauguration from Dwight D. Eisenhower in 1952 to Barack Obama in 2008, spoke all over the world to student, military, and civic organizations. On the 50th anniversary of D-Day, he returned to France, where he joined President Bill Clinton and others in commemorating the event.

Ehlers died in 2014 at the age of 92 and was survived by his wife, Dorothy, two daughters, a son, eleven grandchildren, and two great-grandchildren.

Dorothy said he never bragged about his wartime heroics. On official occasions, when he donned the medal, he always made sure to tell people, "I wear it for all those who didn't come home."

THE MATCHBOX BOAT

LIEUTENANT ROBERT MCPHAIL
AND HIS CREW
Coast Guard Cutter 16

Above the noise of explosions and shelling and machine gun fire, Lieutenant Robert McPhail could hear the shrill cries of men floundering in the water:

"Help me! Help me!"

"I can't stay up much longer!"

"Save me! Please, please, please! I'm hurt!"

Wherever he looked from the pilothouse of CGC-16—the 83-foot coast guard cutter that he commanded—McPhail saw thrashing men pleading for rescue. While dodging artillery shells, underwater obstacles, and machine gun fire from shore, he and his crew of 15 kept plucking men out of the bloody water.

The worst horror for the 29-year-old skipper was seeing the enormous number of bodies floating facedown in the waves. To get to the living, his cutter had to steer through the dead.

Just weeks earlier, CGC-16 had been patrolling off the eastern seaboard of the United States, one of 60 such coast guard cutters based from Maine to Key West, Florida, defending against any possible enemy submarines. But then McPhail and the other commanders of the antisub fleet received secret orders to steam to New York. There, they learned they would become seagoing Saint Bernards, tasked with rescuing troops from stricken landing craft during the Normandy invasion. There were so many dangers facing Allied vessels—mines, torpedoes, enemy shore batteries, landing obstacles, and possible collisions—that military leaders decided rescue boats would be needed.

To add speed and make room for survivors, each cutter was stripped of excess gear, equipment, and all heavy antisubmarine armament. Crews rigged scramble nets to the sides so survivors in the water could climb aboard. Heavy iron davits with block and tackle were fitted on to the deck to lift the wounded.

The cutters were loaded onto convoy ships and transported to Poole, Dorset, England, where they formed Rescue Flotilla One (ResFlo-1 for short) under the direction of Lieutenant Commander Alexander Stewart. Each cutter was furnished with well-stocked first aid chests, extra stretchers, and hundreds of blankets. Every officer and crewmember took classes morning, noon, and night to learn all phases of emergency care. Each cutter was equipped with special self-inflating rubber life rafts that could be tossed in the water to keep groups of survivors afloat while the vessel tried to save others who needed immediate rescue.

Thirty cutters, including CGC-16, were assigned to the US sector of Omaha and Utah Beaches while the other 30 were slated to assist British and Canadian forces at Gold, Sword, and Juno Beaches. Once the vessels rescued troops, they were to bring them to three coast guard–manned naval transports that had been turned into hospital ships and would be anchored eight miles offshore—the USS *Joseph T. Dickman*, the USS *Bayfield*, and the USS *Samuel Chase*.

"Be nothing but a lifeguard," McPhail told his crew the night before the invasion. "We are not here to destroy anything or to kill anybody. We are here just to do rescue operations. And, yes, it will be dangerous because we will be saving lives under heavy enemy fire."

He didn't mention the flotilla's nickname—the "Matchbox Fleet"—even though everyone knew it. Each cutter was built from wood and carried nearly 2,000 gallons of highly flammable fuel in her tank, so if struck by an incendiary grenade, a few well-placed bullets, or an artillery shell, she would go up in flames like a lit matchbox—thus, the nickname.

As his ship left the dock, McPhail thought of his pregnant wife, Elaine, back home in Weaverville, North Carolina. Her due date was only two weeks away. He didn't care if his first-born was a boy or a girl; he just wanted to survive the invasion so one day soon he could hold the baby in his arms.

Around 4:45 a.m. on D-Day, several miles off the Normandy coast, the transport ships began lowering into the water smaller landing craft, which were packed with troops, vehicles, and equipment. Waiting for the signal to charge toward the beaches, the vessels circled around their mother ships as the big guns of nearby battleships, cruisers, and destroyers began their booming barrages of the enemy's seaside defenses. To the Coasties, who had never experienced battle before, the concussive blasts from these guns felt as if they would yank their clothes off.

McPhail noticed that the cutter's flag was twisted around the mast. Before he had a chance to order a crewman to untangle it, Specialist 1st Class Carter Barber climbed the mast and freed the banner. "Well done, Barber," the skipper said.

The first assault wave was now underway. As the 60 cutters of ResFlo-1 fanned out and trailed the landing crafts, McPhail admired how they were knifing through the waves toward their assigned beaches in such orderly rows. But at first light, when the Germans began firing at the invaders, the once-even lines quickly changed into a mishmash of paths. In the noisy, frenzied battle, boats were veering every which way to avoid obstacles, shelling, and wreckage. Direct hits from artillery and struck submerged mines sent many landing craft to watery graves.

After a small landing craft was annihilated by a violent blast, McPhail directed his cutter to the scene, but the crew couldn't find a single survivor, only mangled bodies.

From about 800 yards offshore, LCF-31, a landing craft that had been converted into an antiaircraft vessel, was firing at the opposing enemy gun emplacements just above the beach when an artillery shell struck her. The explosion opened a gaping hole in the hull and pitched dozens of men into the water.

With LCF-31 in flames and sinking rapidly, CGC-16 rushed to her aid. As the cutter closed in on the damaged craft, McPhail and his men passed troops floating facedown in the water.

"Sir, do you want me to stop for them?" the helmsman asked.

"No, let's concentrate on picking up anyone showing signs of life," McPhail replied. And so the cutter weaved through the corpses to reach men bobbing in the water and struggling to keep their heads above the surface. All were begging for help.

"Hang on, boys!" shouted Barber, who was leaning over the railing near the bow. "We're coming!"

One of the men in the water blurted, "I can't stay up!" Exhausted, he repeated, "I can't stay up!"

Barber hurled a heaving line in the man's direction, but it wasn't long enough to reach him, and he sank out of sight. Meanwhile, Coasties were flinging lines into the water to those survivors who were closer to the cutter. Like fishermen on a boat catching a school of fish, the crewmen began pulling in bloody, oil-soaked survivors.

But the strong current and fickle winds punished many troops in the water. Just as the soldiers were about to snare a line, they would be dragged out of reach by the current and wind. Those who didn't have the strength to fight through nature's forces drowned. Some of the others in the water succumbed to fatal wounds.

The rescue operation put the Coasties into the line of fire, but they were resolute in saving lives, even after one of their mates suffered a shrapnel wound when an artillery shell exploded off the starboard bow.

Barber reeled to the side of the boat a heavyset soldier who cried out, "I can't climb the netting. Both my legs are broken."

Because the soldier was about 250 pounds and was weighed down by his waterlogged clothing, helmet, rifle, backpack, and ammunition, it was impossible for Barber alone to haul him aboard. "I need ten pair of hands!" Barber yelled. Several mates came over, and, together, pulled the soldier up and onto the deck. Because there were many others to rescue and time was crucial, they left him lying there in agony.

Troops suffering from wounds, exhaustion, or exposure to the cold water were too weak to hold on to the heaving lines, prompting McPhail, who was also throwing out ropes, to order his men, "If you can't save them with a rope, jump in and get them."

Without hesitation, several Coasties wearing life vests tied lifelines around their waists and leaped into the frigid water. They swam to those missing an arm or leg or were blinded and were close to drowning. The crewmen brought them to the side of the cutter, where fellow mates helped them up the netting.

Out of the 72 men aboard LCF-31, McPhail and his men rescued all who had survived the explosion—18.

After having an ugly gash on his head wrapped, 19-year-old Leonard "Larry" Lampton, who worked in the engine room of the landing craft, told Barber, "It was awful. I was belowdecks when I heard someone shout, 'Shell bursts off the starboard bow!' And then, 'Shell bursts off the port bow!' And then, boom, and everything went black. No lights and lots of smoke. I couldn't see my hands in front of me. I lost consciousness and when I recovered, I found myself underwater. I was scared. Lady Luck was with me, though, because I found an emergency escape hatch, although I really had to struggle to get out."

At roughly the same time that LCF-31 was fatally struck, patrol craft PC-1261 was already sinking about a mile off Utah Beach. As a control vessel, she had been leading a group of landing craft toward a specific spot but moving slowly so they could keep up with her. Zeroing in on her, German shore batteries opened up, landing two rounds a few yards off her bow. Her captain, Lieutenant Commander Rency Sewell, suspected the enemy had figured out her range, which meant the next salvo would likely find its mark. Even though he feared his ship was doomed, he refused to change course because the landing craft following her were relying on her lead.

As expected, a large-caliber shell slammed into PC-1261's engine room, killing 14 of her 65-man crew and wounding many more. The blast tore open the hull, allowing water to pour in. Before the men could do anything to stop the flooding, the boat began listing to starboard. As the badly damaged ship veered off course from the impact, Sewell ordered "all ahead full," hoping to get her out of the way of the landing craft behind her. With her bow dipping even with the surface, she went as far as she could before the flooding in her forward compartments lifted the propellers out of the water.

Knowing there was no way to save her, Sewell ordered everyone to abandon ship. Some jumped into the water while others took to life rafts. Minutes later, PC-1261 capsized, making her the first US Navy ship lost on D-Day. About a dozen survivors managed to climb onto a small section of the overturned hull that was barely above water.

At the time, it was impossible for any of the cutters from ResFlo-1 to pick up the survivors because the Coasties needed to stay out of the way of the initial assault wave. The survivors understood that. In fact, many in rafts were cheering the troops as they passed by in their landing craft.

The closest rescue boat was CGC-16, but it was busy saving the men from LCF-31. After her survivors were brought aboard, McPhail guided his cutter toward the capsized PC-1261, even though his boat was already near capacity with 18 survivors in addition to his crew.

The Coasties ignored the repeated shelling from shore and began picking up the new batch of survivors. CGC-16's skipper, boatswains, gunners, machinist mates, and seamen were tossing out lifelines. Once again, many of McPhail's men braved the cold water and dangerous currents to rescue the seriously wounded.

Now there were nearly 70 troops crammed on the cutter

from bow to stern, including eight casualties in the tiny pilot-house. They were too weak to stand, so they lay on the floor, making it difficult for the crew to move about the cabin. The cramped engine room, which was the warmest spot on the boat, became the "thawing room" for those suffering from hypothermia. Others crowded into the crew's small quarters, where they were jammed three to a bunk. Several Coasties gave their own clothing to survivors to keep them warm and dry.

To make more space, the crew piled survivors' gear and clothing around the boat's 20mm gun mount. The heap—which included heavy jackets, weatherproof clothing, coveralls, underwear, socks, helmets, and gas masks—eventually grew to 5 feet high, 10 feet long, and 10 feet wide. The crew also gathered personal belongings, such as wallets, money, pictures, pocket Bibles, and identification cards and kept them in a safe place. Rifles, carbines, and automatic pistols were stacked below.

All hands—including the ship's cook, 19-year-old George Banks—abandoned their regular duties to either rescue survivors or tend to the wounded. Banks left his galley range and became the makeshift medical officer in charge, telling his comrades, "We're all too busy to get hungry, so I'm not starting any lunch today."

He opened the medical locker and doled out first aid supplies. Relying on the training he received in the weeks leading up to D-Day, Banks began treating men who were suffering from broken legs, split heads, sprained backs, and smashed ankles. He applied tourniquets to stop the bleeding of those who were losing dangerous amounts of blood. Using his sharpest bread knife, he slashed wet clothes off them and covered them with blankets. He put life jackets under them to keep their heads from banging on the deck as the boat bounced from the choppy water and from the shock of exploding shells.

Because the cutter couldn't speed to a hospital-equipped transport ship until all the survivors were rescued, Banks injected morphine into the most serious casualties to help them through the long wait. He then marked "morphine" on their forehead with a wax pencil so they wouldn't get an overdose. Also, it was a way to let the doctors on the transport know who received the drug.

"It was like a mirage, seeing your cutter come out from behind the smoke and confusion," survivor Ralph Tegarten told Barber. Unaware of ResFlo-1, Tegarten added, "Of all the things I expected to find off the coast of Normandy, the last one was the coast guard."

Another rescued man, Tom Weston, a 28-year-old pharmacist's mate and the only medic on PC-1261, sustained a swollen bruise on his head, a black eye, and a laceration on his back. Weston, who was covered in diesel oil, told Barber about the explosion. "There was a crash and a rumble of gear falling around the deck below me," Weston said. "I was knocked down but scrambled to my feet. One shoe was blown off my foot. The ship immediately listed to starboard.

"A young seaman came sliding toward me. As I grabbed

him, he cried, 'My eyes! I can't see!' I explained to him he just had a bad cut on his forehead, and the blood had run into his eyes. When our boat was turning turtle, we slid into the water."

Pointing to his crewmate Everett Keffer, whose ankles had been shattered in the blast, Weston said, "I grabbed hold of Keffer to keep him from drowning because he couldn't swim. We were in the water for quite a while. Somehow, we got into a life raft and then we just held on, hoping we wouldn't get shot or blown up. We saw a landing craft right near us get blasted to pieces. And a plane flying in formation exploded and spun in flames straight into the water. We felt so helpless."

"When we were in the water, I wondered if we would survive," Keffer admitted. "Every time an army landing craft went past us, I'd yell, 'Pick us up! Pick us up!' And they would see me and say, 'Stay strong! We'll go get 'em for you!'"

"It's a good thing you waited for the coast guard," Weston said. "If the army had picked you up, you'd be on Utah Beach right now."

After the last man from PC-1261 was rescued, McPhail ordered the cutter to head toward the *Dickman*, the converted hospital ship. But no sooner had CGC-16 revved up her engines than a small landing craft blew up only a few hundred yards away after hitting an underwater mine. Seeing troops flailing in the water, McPhail told his helmsman, "I don't know where we're going to put them, but we have to rescue those survivors."

CGC-16 sped to the sinking craft. Like before, several Coasties jumped into the water and towed casualties to the cutter. Ten, twenty, thirty, then thirty-five more men—many of them seriously wounded—were brought onboard while the survivors from the other two sunken vessels made room. CGC-16 now had more than five times the number of survivors she was supposed to carry—a whopping 104.

"Skipper, we're packed tighter than a can of tuna," his helmsman said. "Unless some of us hang off the side on the netting, you can't get another man on here."

McPhail agreed and said, "Let's get these boys to the *Dickman*."

The stretcher cases on the exposed deck were covered with blankets to protect them from the soaking spray as CGC-16 plowed through the waves and swerved out of the way of incoming landing craft. After the rescue boat reached the large transport ship, doctors boarded the cutter to examine the stretcher cases and determine who should be taken off first for emergency treatment. One of the physicians pointed to a severely burned soldier and told McPhail, "He's dead." Motioning to another unconscious soldier with a terrible abdominal wound, the doctor said, "He's not going to make it. There's nothing we can do for him."

The dead man and the dying soldier were placed in the lazarette—a storage area near the stern—until they could be buried at sea. The walking wounded limped up the *Dickman*'s gangplank with the uninjured survivors, some of whom were helping carry the casualties.

After boarding the hospital ship, Weston told the medical officer, "I'm a pharmacist's mate, and I want to help in any way I can."

Looking at Weston's bandaged wounds, the officer shook his head and said, "Go take a shower and get all that diesel oil off of you. And then hit the sack [bed] in sick bay. You need to take care of your own wounds." Weston required the assistance of two seamen to wash off the oil.

After the last of the survivors was safely aboard the *Dickman*, crewmen in the transport lowered a piece of steel onto the cutter's deck for use in a burial-at-sea ceremony. McPhail's men mustered by the railing and took off their steel helmets. After reading from a Bible, the skipper motioned for two crewmen to slide the body over the railing. As the corpse splashed into the water and disappeared, McPhail said, "Amen." Several men crossed themselves.

All paused for a moment of silence, which was then broken when the dying soldier—the one who was supposedly beyond hope—pushed open the hatch of the lazarette and, in a hoarse voice, announced, "If you guys think you're gonna do to me what you just did to him, you've got another thing comin'. How about some hot coffee?" Once everyone recovered from their shock, he was rushed over to the *Dickman*.

CGC-16 then motored back toward the beaches. Banks planned to brew coffee for his shipmates, but to reach the stove, he had to remove the wet clothes that survivors in the galley had discarded for dry ones. The soggy apparel had been left on tables, counters, and dish racks, and in the sink and even in the oven. Banks didn't get to deliver the coffee. Just as it began to percolate, he heard over the loudspeaker, "All hands on deck!"

The cutter was nearing LCT-777, a landing craft that was carrying tanks, jeeps, and supplies. She was burning and sinking about 1,500 yards offshore after an explosion from an underwater mine. Under McPhail's direction, CGC-16 came alongside the listing, smoking craft so that those who weren't seriously wounded wouldn't have far to swim to the cutter.

As the Coasties helped survivors aboard, Barber sprinted to the pilothouse and told McPhail, "Sir, one of the LCT guys told me that she's loaded with ammunition. If the fire reaches the ammo, she'll blow sky high and take us with her."

The skipper urged everyone to work faster to complete the evacuation and rescue. Just when he thought it was over, he learned four men were trapped under the remains of a destroyed gun turret and were too injured to free themselves. McPhail nudged his cutter closer to the tilting side of the sinking LCT. It was a risky maneuver because both vessels were swaying in the rough water, and if they crashed, the much smaller cutter faced serious damage. Even more of a concern for the skipper was the possibility that the listing LCT would tip over onto his boat, pinning her and shoving her beneath the surface.

McPhail, however, was intent on saving those men, so he brought the cutter alongside the LCT. Several crewmen climbed aboard the crippled craft and, with the help of ropes, managed to free the four seriously injured troops and bring them safely onto CGC-16.

As the cutter was pulling away, one of the survivors shouted to McPhail, "Skipper, there's still another man on the LCT! Both his legs are severed. I promised I'd get him help. We can't leave him behind!"

McPhail looked at the flames that were steadily advancing across the deck toward the stern, where the large cases of ammo were stored. "We have only a few minutes to rescue him before that boat either explodes or turns turtle," he told the crew.

The cutter once again repositioned next to the LCT. Without waiting for any command, coxswain Arthur Burkhard, Jr., jumped into the water, even though he didn't know how to swim. After splashing around, he grabbed a line tied to the railing of the LCT and climbed aboard. He found the wounded sailor, whose injured legs had tourniquets on them to keep him from bleeding out. The sailor was too weak to talk, but when he saw Burkhard, he smiled.

"I'm going to get you out of here," Burkhard said. The Coastie placed a line around the sailor's waist as heavy smoke and flames streamed out of the open hatches. Burkhard carried the sailor to the railing, but he couldn't lower him on the rope to the cutter below because the LCT was listing at a steep angle and was about to crush the rescue boat. McPhail had to back CGC-16 away.

"Listen," Burkhard told the sailor. "I know this is going to sound terribly cruel, but I'm going to throw you in the water. It's the only way to save you."

The sailor looked at him with trusting eyes and nodded.

Burkhard pushed him off the LCT's deck and, after watching him hit the water, jumped in. Seeing what Burkhard had done, two Coasties leaped overboard and towed the sailor to the cutter's netting. They helped him pull himself up hand over hand to the deck. Meanwhile, Burkhard, who was flapping his arms in the water and kicking furiously, grabbed a heaving line tossed by his mates, who yanked him to the netting.

As soon as Burkhard reached the deck of the cutter, the LCT rolled over completely and then, gurgling loudly, sank.

Now wrapped in a blanket, Burkhard checked on the sailor, who was silently watching two crewmen cut off his clothes, apply fresh tourniquets to what was left of his legs, and administer morphine. When he saw Burkhard, the sailor gave him a wink and then passed out.

"He is the bravest man I've seen today," Burkhard said to his shipmates. "He never whined or moaned or complained. He kept himself under control and was smiling the whole time."

The crew of CGC-16 had rescued 22 men off the LCT, 19 of whom were in serious condition. With no other nearby vessels in distress at the moment, the cutter delivered her newest group of survivors to the *Dickman*.

By now, McPhail and his crew were whipped mentally and physically, but proud. On this memorable day, they had saved

126 men. Thanks to the Coasties' training and dedication, they had kept alive all but one of the most gravely wounded, including those who had lost limbs.

Following the latest rescue, Banks returned to the galley, where he boiled peas and baked pork chops, potatoes, and a raisin pie. While hungrily devouring Banks's cooking, some shipmates discovered Burkhard wasn't aware that the LCT-777 had been carrying a large amount of ammunition. When told that the vessel would have exploded from the flames if she hadn't capsized first, Burkhard said, "It's a good thing I didn't know about that ammo. I would have been twice as scared as I already was."

CGC-16 rescued more men on D-Day than any other cutter in Rescue Flotilla One. Each member of the crew was awarded the Bronze Star and the Navy and Marine Corps Medal for gallantry. In addition to receiving the latter medal, Lieutenant Robert McPhail earned the Silver Star for his heroism.

The entire Matchbox Fleet of 60 cutters performed magnificently on D-Day and in the following weeks, rescuing 1,438 persons, including a British nurse on a hospital ship that sank after hitting a mine. More than 500 of those rescued were saved during the first 36 hours of the invasion. Reports indicated that about half the survivors picked up during the first two days were either seriously wounded or had suffered from shock.

Other than the CGC-16 crewmember who sustained a shrapnel wound, no Coastie had any serious injuries, and only two cutters were lost when they ran aground during a storm two weeks after D-Day. "We found out later that there was an anticipated two-thirds casualty rate for us," Carter Barber wrote afterward. "Most of us weren't expected to make it, but we all did. We didn't think we were being heroic because we were just doing what we had to do."